Mary

Icon of Trinitarian Love

Anthony J Kelly CSsR

Mary

Icon of Trinitarian Love

Anthony J Kelly CSsR

Adelaide
2022

A Forum for Theology in the World
Volume 9, Issue 2, 2022

A Forum for Theology in the World is an academic refereed journal aimed at engaging with issues in the contemporary world, a world which is pluralist and ecumenical in nature. The journal reflects this pluralism and ecumenism. Each edition is theme specific and has its own editor responsible for the production. The journal aims to elicit and encourage dialogue on topics and issues in contemporary society and within a variety of religious traditions. The Editor in Chief welcomes submissions of manuscripts, collections of articles, for review from individuals or institutions, which may be from seminars or conferences or written specifically for the journal. An internal peer review is expected before submitting the manuscript. It is the expectation of the publisher that, once a manuscript has been accepted for publication, it will be submitted according to the house style to be found at the back of this volume. All submissions to the Editor in Chief are to be sent to: hdregan@ atf. org.au.

Each edition is available as a journal subscription, or as a book in print, pdf or epub, through the ATF Press web site — www.atfpress.com. Journal subscriptions are also available through EBSCO and other library suppliers.

Editor in Chief
Hilary Regan, ATF Press

A Forum for Theology in the World is published by ATF Theology and imprint of ATF (Australia) Ltd (ABN 90 116 359 963) and is published twice or three times a year.

ISBN: 978-1-923006-04-1 soft
         978-1-923006-05-8 hard
         978-1-923006-06-5 epub
         978-1-923006-07-2 pdf

SCAN ME

Published and edited by

THEOLOGY

Making a lasting impact

An imprint of the ATF Press Publishing Group
owned by ATF (Australia) Ltd.
PO Box 234
Brompton, SA 5007
Australia
ABN 90 116 359 963
www.atfpress.com

A Forum for Theology in the World Vol 9 No 2/2022

Table of Contents

Foreword   vii
     Dorothy Lee

1.   Mary Icon of Trinitarian Love   1

2.   Mary and the Heart   29

3.   The Assumption of Mary   43

4.   May Marian Procession   47

5.   Mary: From Image to Reality   53

6.   Mary, Icon of Trinitarian Love—The God-bearer   65

7.   Mary and a Poet—Gerard Manley Hopkins   83

Foreword

The place of Mary in Christian theology has been a contested one, ever since the Protestant Reformation of the sixteenth century and also the advent of feminist theology in the twentieth century. Protestantism challenged much of the Mediaeval piety surrounding Mary in the West, along with her intercessory role and that of the saints more generally. Feminist thinking has questioned the portrayal of Mary as the demure and passive virgin-mother, a portrayal that places her beyond the ken of ordinary women.

In all this turmoil of questioning and dispute, including effects on the ecumenical front to find common ground in the figure of Mary (ARCIC), Anthony Kelly has produced a very fine and moving series of reflections on the person and theological significance of Mary. Writing from a Roman Catholic perspective, Fr Kelly points to Mary's role in elucidating the core doctrines of the faith: the Trinity, the church, the sacraments (particularly the Eucharist), and eschatology. He sees Mary's role in the life of the church, from beginning to end, as pervasive. Her presence weaves through every point in the church's existence, in its origins, its ongoing ministry and mission, and its final goal.

I write in response to Fr Kelly's reflections as an Anglican priest, with a special interest in the New Testament, particularly the Gospels. As an Anglican committed to the *via media*, I am conscious of very different voices in my denomination. On the one hand, those on the more Protestant side tend to discount Mary, concerned that she seems to take over the role of Christ or the Holy Spirit, almost approaching the godhead. This view sometimes accompanies the discounting of the place and significance of all women as disciples of Christ in the early Christian movement.

Some feminists within the Protestant tradition, who do not wish to discount women as disciples, nevertheless sometimes question her virginity and dismiss its place in her theological portraiture. They want instead to confirm Mary's place within the ranks of the many Galilean women in the Gospels who follow Jesus and minister to him.

On the other side, I am equally aware of voices that say the opposite: who long to recover a truly 'catholic' sense of Mary to Anglicanism. Here the emphasis is on Mary as the *Theotokos*, the God-bearer, the source and guarantor of the incarnation. For Anglicanism on this more 'catholic' side, the incarnation is the centre of its Christology, and to that Mary bears supreme witness in her body and with her whole-hearted faith. In this respect, there is a kind of transcendence to Mary's person, a quality that makes her iconic and a means by which we can apprehend and experience God. In Fr Kelly's words, 'Her face is not a mirror reflecting back our own image, but more a window through which the light of an arresting otherness breaks through.'

For Anglican feminists within this more 'catholic' tradition, Mary plays a unique role in God's salvation, co-operating with God as a woman in the fulfillment of the divine plan in Christ. Her *fiat* represents her courageous and bold self-gift to God which becomes a model for the Christian community, male as well as female. Portrayals of her from the early church as priest are particularly powerful in this ancient yet re-conceived view of Mary, and she has become for many women priests an icon of priesthood who supports and prays for them in their vocation.

This feminist perspective within orthodox Anglicanism focusses particularly on the witness of the Gospels and their presentation of Mary. It emphasises Mary's prime place among the many Galilean women whom the Gospel of Luke presents as disciples, witnesses and ministers (Lk 8:1–3). She is the first Christian in Luke's Gospel and, in the Acts of the Apostles, Luke's second volume, she is present at Pentecost (Acts 1:14) where she too receives the Holy Spirit, with the tongues of fire and the capacity for inspired speech.

At the same time, within the Gospels, Mary stands shoulder-to-shoulder with another prominent female disciple: Mary Magdalene, whose name is most likely a nick-name given her by Jesus: Mary 'the Tower' (Lk 8:2). She is never portrayed as a prostitute or sinful woman but is rather the witness to the resurrection, just as Mary the mother of Jesus bears witness to the incarnation. Both women together represent not only the discipleship but also the leadership of women, alongside the Twelve, within the early Christian community. A renewed emphasis on Mary the Mother of God places her alongside the concomitant role of Mary, the Apostle of the Apostles.

For Anglicans, there remain other difficult and controversial issues around Mary, particularly relating to her immaculate conception and perpetual virginity. It strikes me that both notions are problematical from a biblical and theological point of view. If Mary is conceived without sin, how then can she call on God as her 'Saviour' in the Magnificat (Lk 1:47)? How do we respond to her misunderstanding of Jesus' ministry in Mark's Gospel when she and her family want to protect the family honour by removing him from conflict with the religious authorities, and when he claims, not her and his siblings, but his disciples as his true family (Mk 3:31–35)? None of this is to deny other points in the Gospel where Mary displays her undoubted goodness and strength of faith (Lk 1:38, Jn 2:5), but to ascribe to her the kind of sinless humanity that is characteristic of her Son (see Heb 4:15) seems to have no strong basis in Scripture and potentially challenges the uniqueness of Jesus as the divinely human Son, Wisdom and Word of God.

Within this framework, the notion of virginity can also be problematical. I see no problem in affirming the virginal conception of Jesus which is independently attested to in both Matthew and Luke (Matt 1:18–20; Luke 1:34–35). Moreover, the virginal conception means that Jesus has a uniquely female-oriented humanity, dependent only (humanly speaking) on his mother. This factor might well account for Jesus' extraordinary capacity in his ministry to speak to women as fully human: without demeaning them or raising them on a pedestal. It may also explain why so many women flocked to his ministry and became his followers. But why should the virginal conception extend to Mary's perpetual virginity? The most obvious meaning of Matthew 1:25 is that Mary goes on to have other children and a normal sexual relationship with Joseph. Otherwise, we are in danger of implying that sexual intimacy is in some sense problematical (which some of the early church writers believed).

Oddly enough—and perhaps this is my inconsistency—I have least problems with the doctrine of the assumption. It simply places Mary, as representing the church, in the same place where we will all find ourselves: raised body and soul into God's new heaven and new earth in the resurrection. It is not, to my mind, indicated in the New Testament writings (except perhaps for the heavenly woman in Revelation 12 which, these days, we tend to read as an image of Israel rather than Mary). On the other hand, the assumption is not denied in the New Testament or inconsistent with it, and could be said to represent a trajectory from the biblical text. It makes sense in the light of passages such as Paul's discussion of the future, material resurrection of the dead (1 Cor 15:35–49).

These are small reservations in the grand scheme of things: attempts to balance the boat from an Anglican perspective. They do not detract from the beauty of Fr Kelly's prose or his deep insights into the person and mission of Mary, including her eschatological significance. I found much to love and learn from in his writings and I warmly commend this book to the reader. It is stimulating and beautiful, and gives a high place to this wondrous woman who had the courage to bear God in her body and in her heart, and who continues to pray with us and for us in the heavenly courts until we join her and all the saints, female and male, in God's final kingdom.

Revd Prof Dorothy A Lee FAHA
Trinity College
University of Divinity

Further Reading:

The Anglican-Roman Catholic International Commission. *Mary, Grace and Hope in Christ: An Agreed Statement* https://www.anglicancommunion.org/media/105263/mary-grace-and-hope-in-christ_english.pdf

Bauckham, Richard, *Gospel Women: Studies of the Named Women in the Gospels* (Grand Rapids: Eerdmans, 2002).

Cohick, Lynn. *Women in the World of the Earliest Christians: Illuminating Ancient Ways of Life* (Grand Rapids: Baker Academic, 2009).

Gaventa, Beverly Roberts. *Mary: Glimpses of the Mother of Jesus*. Studies on Personalities of the New Testament (Columbia: University of South Carolina Press, 1995).

Johnson, Elizabeth, *Truly Our Sister: A Theology of Mary in the Communion of Saints* (New York: Continuum, 2003).

Kateusz, Ally. *Mary and Early Christian Women: Hidden Leadership* (Cham, Switzerland: Palgrave Macmillan, 2019).

Lee, Dorothy, *The Ministry of Women in the New Testament: Reclaiming the Biblical Vision for Church Leadership* (Eugene, OR: Baker Academic, 2021).

Moloney, Francis J, *Mary: Woman and Mother* (Eugene, OR: Wipf & Stock, 2009).

Sayers, Dorothy L, 'The Human-Not-Quite-Human', in *Unpopular Opinions*, 121–22. London: Victor Gollancz, 1946.

Joan Taylor, 'Missing Magdala and the Name of Mary "Magdalene"' *Palestine Exploration Quarterly* 146 (2014): 205–223. https://www.researchgate.net/publication/278323992_Missing_magdala_and_the_name_of_mary_%27magdalene%27

Mary: Icon of Trinitarian Love[1]

Abstract:

> This article argues that the presence of Mary to Christian faith
> can be helpfully considered as a 'saturated phenomenon' (Jean-
> Luc Marion). Inseparable from the Christ-Event, the Marian
> phenomenon affects faith's perception of the self-revelation of
> God. It is theologically illumined by reflecting on the seven
> key terms that are essential to the Christian story: Father, Son,
> Holy Spirit, Cross, Resurrection, Church and Eternal Life.

The Marian presence in Christian life is a manifold phenomenon—
in scripture, liturgy, doctrine, devotion, art, spirituality,[2] personal
witness and theological traditions, not to mention apparitions and
special places of pilgrimage. In Catholic parlance, this compact,
multifaceted and intensely personal presence is often referred to as
the 'mystery of Mary' in the life of the Church. It cannot be separated
from what Paul speaks of as 'the mystery that has been hidden
throughout the ages and generations but has now been revealed to
his [God's] saints . . . Christ in you, the hope of glory' (Col 1:26–27).

---

1. This is an extensive reworking of an article originally appearing under the title,
   'Mary and the Creed: Icon of Trinitarian Love', in *Irish Theological Quarterly*, 69
   (2004): 17–30. I am grateful to the editor of the aforesaid journal for permission
   to revise the article concerned and to develop it further.
2. The number of male and female religious orders/ congregations is a massive
   phenomenon in its own right. Examples are close at hand: the Marists (the
   different Societies of Fathers, Brothers, and Sisters), The Institute of the Blessed
   Virgin Mary, The Presentation Sisters, the Sisters of Mercy, the Oblates of Mary
   Immaculate, the Servites—where do we stop, since practically every known
   religious order/congregation boasts of a Marian inspiration?

Doctrinal language refers to the 'mysteries of faith'—the Trinity, incarnation, grace and the beatific vision. These are the revealed objects of faith, since reason unaided could not deduce them. On a more devotional level, there are the 'mysteries' of the life of our Lord. Various aspects of Christian revelation become the subject of contemplation—as in the once fifteen, and now twenty, 'mysteries of the Rosary'.[3] On a more theological plane, say in the theology of Karl Rahner, 'mystery' is fundamental notion expressive of God's self-communication to the human spirit.[4] The mystery in this sense is not something to be solved, but something so given, and so radically self-giving, that it constitutes the basic horizon of life and existence itself. Consequently, all the 'mysteries' of faith are aspects of the one self-giving mystery of God which, even as it communicates itself in the Word and Spirit, remains ever beyond any finite grasp. Even in the beatific vision of God face-to-face, the inexhaustible infinities of the divine reality are not comprehended. In that final vision, the divine mystery is not lessened in the life of the blessed, but more positively appreciated in its boundless excess.

In this perspective, the mystery of Mary in the life of the People of God can be helpfully appreciated as 'saturated phenomenon' (Jean-Luc Marion). It so permeates Christian consciousness as to demand a special kind of receptivity appropriate to the gift of revelation itself. Christian theology, through it is 'faith seeking understanding', can get lost in refined conceptualism and systematic control unless it is phenomenologically grounded in a 'faith receptive to the distinctiveness of what has been so given'. There is an 'excess' of the divine self-giving that overflows and disrupts the mundane routines of human experience and rational control.

In line with such a phenomenological perspective, this article is presented in four main sections:

---

3. John Paul II, *Rosarium Virginis Mariae*, <http://www.vatican.va/holy_father/john_paul_ii/apost_letters/documents/hf_jp-ii_apl_20021016_rosarium-virginis-mariae_en.html>

4. For a seminal article, see Karl Rahner, 'The Concept of Mystery in Catholic Theology', *Theological Investigations IV*, translated by Kevin Smyth (Baltimore, MD: Helicon Press, 1966), 36–73.

1. A phenomenologically attuned theology of Mary;[5]
2. Doctrinal Development: The Marian Catalyst;
3. Key Terms in the Marian phenomenon;
4. Seven evocative correlations.

A Phenomenologically Attuned Theology of Mary

Fundamental to a phenomenological approach is receptivity to what is given on its own terms. It must be allowed to impose itself on the consciousness of faith in its own singularity. Whether it is the Christian phenomenon as a whole, or the place of Mary within it, what has been *so* given, must be allowed to disclose itself in its own way. That is to say that the phenomenon, least of all in the realm of faith, does not show itself as already circumscribed by the abstract, systematic generalizations of the rational ego that are already in place. Neither human nor divine possibilities are so pre-established. In the teeming, elusive relativities of the postmodern world, there is an opportunity for Christian faith to show not only the courage of its own convictions, but also to act with a fresh receptivity to the distinctiveness of revelation, and so witness to the prodigal excess of the gift from which it is born.[6]

What has been so given constitutes the *data* for Christian intelligence. More deeply, it is received as the *donum*, the gift, flowing forth from the inexhaustible and ever-continuing self-giving of God in Christ. This prodigality of self-giving saturates every dimension of

---

5. In have treated these points more extensively in *The Resurrection Effect: Transforming Christian Life and Thought* (Maryknoll, NY: Orbis, 2008). As the title implies, the book was primarily focused on the phenomenon of the Resurrection of the Crucified One, but the 'effect' permeates all Christian life and thought. See especially, chapter 2, 'A Phenomenological Approach to the Resurrection', 24–43.

6. Jean-Luc Marion's influential trilogy, *Reduction and Givenness: Investigations of Husserl, Heidegger, and Phenomenology*, translated by Thomas A Carlson (Evanston, IL: Northwestern University Press (1998), *Being Given: Toward a Phenomenology of Givenness*, translated by Jeffrey L Kosky (Stanford, CA: Stanford University Press, 2002), *In Excess: Studies of Saturated Phenomena*, trans. Robyn Horner and Vincent Barraud (New York: Fordham University Press, 2002). For further elaboration and background, see *God Without Being: Hors-Texte*, translated by Thomas A Carlson (Chicago, IL: Chicago University Press, 1991).

Christian life. In the light of the resurrection, Christ gives himself as incarnate among us, present in the gift of the Spirit, and in the word of the inspired Scriptures, in the sacraments of the ecclesial community; and, indeed, through the entire universe transformed in him. This manifold self-giving of Christ contains a particular dimension. He gives his Mother to the Church represented by the Beloved Disciple at the foot of the Cross (Jn 19:26–27).

For the moment, we observe simply that the phenomenality of Mary in the life of the Church is saturated with the singularity of the Christ-event in which she stands. In that horizon of grace, Mary is not an idolic or mythological projection of religious sensibilities. She appears, rather, as an iconic 're-presentation' of the Christocentric focus of Christian existence. Her presence is back-lit, as it were, by the 'light from light', to use the phrase from the Nicene Creed. Her singular place in the event of God's self-giving love affects faith's perception of the truth that is revealed, of the identity it confers, of the community it forms, and of world-renewing praxis it inspires. When the Christian community contemplates the Marian phenomenon in all its dimensions, faith is not distracted from the realm of light inaccessible (1 Tim 6:16). Nor does it turn from the light that shines through the face of Christ (2 Cor 4:6). Rather, the figure of Mary gestures toward the source of light itself. She represents the intentionality of faith in its receptivity to the Christ-event. In the words of Elizabeth's greeting, 'Blessed is she who believed that there would be a fulfilment of what was spoken to her by the Lord' (Lk 1:45). Mary has surrendered to the incalculable significance of what is being revealed, and yielded to its unfolding in time. In her maternal receptivity to God's self-involvement in the world, 'Mary treasured all these words and pondered them in her heart' (Lk 2:19), for 'his mother treasured all these things in her heart' (Lk 2:51). She embodies the heart of faith surrendering to the God for whom 'nothing will be impossible' (Lk 1:37).

For Mary, the mystery is not only in her heart and mind; for she is also *in* it in the wholeness of her being. She is caught up in excess of what is taking place, within the event itself, and participating in its unfolding in history. Given to faith in the saturated phenomenon of Christ, she is 'in Christ' in her uniqueness. She pre-figures the transformatively new: 'if anyone is in Christ, there is a new creation: everything old has passed away; see, everything has become new' (2

Cor 5:17). As the Virgin Mother of Jesus, as Mother of the Church, already possessed by the Holy Spirit, she intimately belongs to this 'new creation'. Though what we shall be is not yet revealed (1 Jn 3:2), the destined transformation of all is anticipated in Mary. As Mother of Christ, head and members, she witnesses to the incalculable rebirth of all in the Spirit. She represents in her person that such a world-changing event is not a time-conditioned *fait accompli*, but an ongoing drama for human freedom. In this regard, she represents the adventure of the Christian vocation, in the deepest meaning of the word, *ad venturum*, literally, 'toward the one who will come'. She stands at the point where human existence has been made open to the imaginable future of 'God all in all' (1 Cor 15:28). She stands, therefore, within the event of God's self-revelation as its servant and witness.[7] In this measure, the event of God's entry into human history shows its 'anarchic', irreducibly original character in the Virgin Mother. She proclaims the grace she has received, witnessing to the God who 'scatters the proud in the thoughts of their hearts', who brings down the powerful from their thrones, exalting the lowly, and filling the hungry with good things (*Cf* Lk 1:48–53).

As the history of Christian art testifies, Mary has inspired the deepest feelings for the beautiful, to give faith's dim apprehension of the glory to be revealed a focus and embodiment. In the divine beauty that plays on her, the mundane house of human experience must be arranged to let in new possibilities. The aesthetic character of God's self-disclosure has provoked refined responses in theological phenomenology.[8] God enters the human world by appealing to the intimations of beauty and longing that stir the human heart. Speaking of art more generally, a noted critic, George Steiner, makes a telling point. To appreciate any work of art, be it a poem, a painting, a sculpture or a great piece of music, we must enter wholly into it and breathe the sense of life it evokes. We do not behold it from the outside, but give ourselves over to entering into the world it depicts. Art transforms

---

7. See Kelly, *The Resurrection Effect*, 29–42 as it calls on Marion, *Being Given*, 234–236.

8. Hans Urs von Balthasar, *The Glory of the Lord. A Theological Aesthetics I: Seeing the Form*, translated by Erasmo Leiva-Merikakis, edited by Joseph Fessio, SJ and John Riches (Edinburgh: T&T Clark, 1982); David Bentley Hart, *The Beauty of the Infinite: The Aesthetics of Christian Truth* (Grand Rapids, MI: Eerdmans, 2003).

consciousness. It reorients our existence by inspiring sensitivities to what has previously been hidden or overlooked. Beauty enacted in art evokes a deeper awareness of the mystery of being and the depths of experience. It has a transformative impact, even as it witnesses to the transcendent. Steiner, a European intellectual of Jewish background, finds in the image of the Annunciation an evocation of aesthetic dimensions usually bracketed out of our routine experience:

> the shorthand image is that of the Annunciation, of "a terrible beauty" or gravity breaking into the small house of our cautionary being. If we have heard rightly the wing-beat and the provocation of that visit, the house is no longer habitable in quite the same way as before. A mastering intrusion has shifted the light . . .[9]

To use Steiner's image, Mary stands at the point where the light shifts, and a larger horizon opens up. When the Angel Gabriel is sent to Mary to announce that she is to be the mother of Jesus, the Messiah, the measure of 'the small house' of our humanly-bounded existence is made open to another presence—the One she is to conceive. Around her gathers the 'terrible beauty' and 'gravity' of God's self-revelation with its 'transformative summons'.

As the Mother of Christ, she is now related to the Church as a unique member of his transformed body of Christ. For from her flesh, Christ was born; and in her flesh, she is united with him in his glory.[10] Her 'body' or 'flesh' is saturated with a special sense of immediacy and unobjectifiable intimacy with her Son, a field communication with God, in mutual indwelling and self-disclosure. Her whole bodily

---

9. George Steiner, *Real Presences* (Chicago: Chicago University Press, 1996), 143.
10. John Paul II, *Redemptoris Mater*:

> Mary, as the Mother of Christ, is in a particular way united with the Church, 'which the Lord established as his own body' . . . It is significant that the conciliar text places this truth about the Church as the Body of Christ . . . in close proximity to the truth that the Son of God "through the power of the Holy Spirit was born of the Virgin Mary." The reality of the Incarnation finds a sort of extension in the mystery of the Church-the Body of Christ. And one cannot think of the reality of the Incarnation without referring to Mary, the Mother of the Incarnate Word (n 5).
> <<http://www.vatican.va/holy_father/john_paul_ii/encyclicals/documents/hf_jp-ii_enc_25031987_redemptoris-mater_en.html>>

being has been re-experienced in the flesh of Christ,[11] to incarnate the form of self-giving love for those who are 'members, one of another' (Eph 4:25), 'for no one ever hates his own flesh, but he nourishes and tenderly care for it, just as Christ does for the church, because we are members of his body' (Eph 5:30). The Letter to the Ephesians does not hesitate to appeal to the most intimate, ecstatic and generative human experience of the body in spousal love to express Christ's relationship to the ecclesial body. Just as man and woman become 'one flesh' (Gn 2:23; Mt 19:6; Mk 10:8), the risen One is one flesh with the community of believers. As the human mother of Jesus, she is 'one flesh' with her son. In the realm of the new creation, she is now 'one flesh' with him in a nuptial sense (*Cf* Gen 2:23; Mt 19:6; Mk 10:8)—for Christ has 'made her holy' (Eph 5:26) and presented her 'to himself in splendour, without spot or wrinkle' (v 27).

When the face of Mary is turned toward the Church, her features reveal something of the invisible totality of Christ, the son she holds within her. Her gaze makes its own demands: 'Do whatever he tells you' (Jn 2:5). Her face is not a mirror reflecting back our own image, but more a window through which the light of an arresting otherness breaks through. Paul speaks expansively of Christ, 'the image of the invisible God' (Col 1:15). It calls forth prayer, adoration and self-surrender. The *eikon* of Christ inspires a waiting and longing for his final appearance, typified in the earliest recorded Christian prayer, Maranatha, 'Come, Lord!' (1 Cor 16:22; Rev 22:20).[12] Mary thus turns to the faithful with the features of one who been found among those who 'look upon the one whom they have pierced' (Jn 19:37). She is an anticipation of the promised 'face to face' vision (1 Cor 13:12), for already the God of light has shone in her heart 'to give the light of the knowledge of the glory of God in the face of Christ' (2 Cor 4:6).

These brief evocations of the 'saturated phenomenon' of Mary in the life of the Church—in relation to the event, the radiance, the flesh, and the face of Christ—have a certain equivalent expression in the Anglican-Roman Catholic document, *Mary: Grace and Hope in Christ* (2004).[13] She is 'the pattern' of grace and hope. She belongs to the 'celebration of important aspects of our common Christian heritage',

---

11. Marion, *Le phénomène érotique*, 185.
12. Marion, *In Excess*, 124.
13. <http://www.vatican.va/roman_curia/pontifical_councils/chrstuni/angl-comm-docs/rc_pc_chrstuni_doc_20050516_mary-grace-hope-christ_en.html>

as the 'exemplar of faithful obedience', the expression of 'grace-filled response' to the divine intention to unite all in the 'body of Christ'. As such, she is 'the figure of the Church' as open in 'receptivity' to the Spirit—a point of 'convergence' in the worship of 'a vast community of love and prayer'.[14] The document looks back to common Christian traditions and the trinitarian and ecclesial dimensions implied.[15] Inherent in such common traditions is the forward-looking 'eschatological' significance of Mary for Christian faith and hope.[16] All such considerations figure in a 're-reception' of Marian doctrine in the interests of a deeper ecumenical consensus. Since this would imply, along with the necessary historical and theological studies, a greater attentiveness to the experiential roots of faith at the level of mind, heart, feeling, imagination and responsibility, I have reflected first on a fresh 'receptivity' to the Marian phenomenon, the better to enable a re-reception on the level of doctrine.

A freshly 'receptive' re-reception becomes necessary when previous forms have become too narrow and ossified. Fundamentalisms, of either devotional or intellectual kinds, bring forth their own kinds of ideological projections and polarisations. The older self-contained

---

14. From *Mary: Grace and Hope in Christ*, Introduction:

> Our Agreed Statement concerning the Blessed Virgin Mary as **pattern** of grace and hope is a powerful reflection of our efforts to seek out what we hold in common and celebrates important aspects of our common **heritage**. Mary, the mother of our Lord Jesus Christ, **stands before us as an exemplar** of faithful obedience, and her 'Be it to me according to your word' is the grace-filled **response** each of us is called to make to God, both personally and communally, as the Church, the **body** of Christ. It is as **figure** of the Church, her arms uplifted in prayer and praise, her hands open in **receptivity** and availability to the outpouring of the Holy Spirit, that we are one with Mary as she magnifies the Lord. 'Surely,' Mary declares in her song recorded in the Gospel of Luke, 'from this day all generations will call me blessed.' [my emphasis]

15. *Mary: Grace and Hope in Christ*:

> This tradition has at its core the proclamation of the Trinitarian 'economy of salvation', grounding the life and faith of the Church in the divine communion of Father, Son and Spirit. We have sought to understand Mary's person and role in the history of salvation and the life of the Church in the light of a theology of divine grace and hope. Such a theology is deeply rooted in the enduring experience of Christian worship and devotion (n 4).

16. *Mary: Grace and Hope in Christ*, n 52.

Mariology of dogmatic theology can no longer be simply retrieved. It is a matter of finding a new focus within a fresh horizon, expansive enough to allow for the convergence of scriptural witness, doctrinal traditions, liturgy, art and devotion in ecclesial faith.

Though attempting a more phenomenological approach to figure of Mary, I am not stopping short at some form of purely aesthetic appreciation of the impact of Mary on Christian consciousness. Hence, the importance of emphasizing that, from beginning to end, Mary is situated within the summons of Christian conversion to the reign of God as Christ proclaimed it. She stands therefore within the salvific economy of God's self-revelation. Within this theocentric focus, a fresh receptivity to the Marian phenomenon will work as a *reprise* and a "re-presentation" of the theological themes embedded in Christian story of grace and salvation, in the particular manner in which she receives and gives. Within this 'trajectory of grace and hope', the entire sweep of salvation history comes into focus: creation, the election of the Chosen People, the incarnation, ministry, death, resurrection and ascension of Christ, the gift of the Spirit in the Church, all leading to eternal life and creation transformed.[17] If Christ is the Yes to all God's promises, and the Amen to all our prayers (2 Cor 1:18–20),[18] Mary appears in the radiance of the divine affirmation of our humanity, just as her *fiat*, 'Be it done unto me according to your word', (Lk 1:38), is a radical endorsement of the Amen of the human surrender to the ways of God.

Doctrinal Development: The Marian Catalyst

While a more refined receptivity to the Marian phenomenon means more than a synthesis of the Church's Marian doctrines, the figure of Mary cannot be abstracted from doctrinal developments and the intertwining of Trinitarian, Christological and ecclesial questions.[19] It was not until the fifth century, in the Council of Ephesus (431), that Mary was declared to be *Theotokos*, the 'God-bearer', the Mother

---

17. *Mary: Grace and Hope in Christ*, n 6.
18. *Mary: Grace and Hope in Christ*, n 5.
19. For a critical evaluation of the emergence of early devotion or 'cult' of the Virgin Mary, a valuable collection of articles is found in *The Origins of the Cult of the Virgin Mary*, edited by Christ Maunder (London: Burns and Oates, 2008).

of God.[20] A huge doctrinal development had been in progress over those five centuries, as is evidenced in the early councils of Nicaea (325), Ephesus (431) and Chalcedon (451). The issue turned on the distinctive truth of Christian faith. How were Christians to speak of the divine reality itself? Was God personally revealed in the incarnation? Was the incarnate Word truly and personally human, or merely gesturing in a figurative humanity? In fact, Christian thinkers, in their various attempts to answer such questions, went some of the way with the great pagan philosophers who had formed the culture in which Christian theology operated. Both Christian theologians and pagan philosophers had one common concern. Both wanted to lay to rest the lurid, polytheistic extravagances of ancient mythologies, and so to concentrate on the one, true, good ultimate reality from which everything came. But the intelligence of faith could not rest there. It had to account for the distinctive reality of what had been revealed; and, to that degree, to go beyond what even the best of what Greek philosophy had to offer. The faith, that through these early centuries had prayed, celebrated, suffered and pondered its mysteries, led to an understanding of God in completely un-Greek terms. Not only was God the creative source of the universe, but lovingly related to the world. There was indeed only one God. However, that one God was never solitary in perfection, but existed in the life of Trinitarian communion, three divine persons inter-related in an eternal vitality. This divine Trinity not only freely created the world, but had lovingly reached into the world in order to draw it into God's own life—so that God would be 'all in all' (1 Cor 15:28).[21] Furthermore, if the revealed God were so self-giving, as Father, Son and Holy Spirit, how must faith speak of the 'self' that God had to give? In the light of Christ's resurrection, everything about God, our world and our humanity— and about Mary—had to be re-evaluated and re-imagined. Indeed, unless Christ had risen from the dead, there would be no New Testament, no Church, no Trinitarian doctrines, and no Marian presence to Christian faith and hope.[22]

---

20. See Richard M Price, 'The *Theotokos* and the Council of Ephesus', in Maunder, *The Origins of the Cult of the Virgin Mary*, 89-104.
21. See Anthony J Kelly, 'Mystery and Definition', in *The Trinity of Love. A Theology of the Christian God* (Wilmington, Del: Michael Glazier, 1989), 59–64.
22. See Kelly, *The Resurrection Effect*, 44–78.

The confession of Mary as *Theotokos* occurred at a vital juncture in the development of Church teaching of the one person of Christ, true God and true man.[23] His humanity was not an apparent or "docetic" humanity, for he was truly born of a human mother—'consubstantial with the Father according to his divinity, and consubstantial with us according to his humanity' (Chalcedon, 451).[24] At the same time, her virginal conception by the Holy Spirit[25] pointed to the divinity of her son—and the unique dignity of Mary's role in the incarnation. Because Christ is one person, Mary was not merely the mother of his humanity, but truly the mother of the divine person who had entered human history: she was the mother of the Word incarnate.[26] In the words of Chalcedon, 'One and the same Son . . . was begotten from the Father before the ages as to the divinity and in the latter days for us and our salvation was born as to the humanity from Mary the Virgin Mother of God'.[27] In this doctrinal development, Mary, as the Virgin-Mother of the Incarnate Word, was understood not as a mythological regression, but as the focal point in the elaboration of the reality of the incarnation.[28]

The confession of Mary as *Theotokos*, as the virginal God-bearer, was both the stimulus and the product of intense theological efforts to clarify what the Church actually believed and meant in its fundamental Trinitarian and Christological faith. In reference to her, the great poem of Christian faith found a doctrinal vocabulary consistent enough to enable it to break free from pagan myths and traditional

---

23. *Mary: Grace and Hope in Christ*, n 31.
24. *The Christian Faith in the Doctrinal Documents of the Catholic Church* (revised edition), edited by Neuner SJ and J Dupuis SJ (London: Collins, 1982), n 614–615.
25. *Mary: Grace and Hope in Christ*, n 33.
26. *Mary: Grace and Hope in Christ*, n 34.
27. *The Christian Faith . . .*, n 624.
28. By the end of the fifth century, commemoration of Mary as 'God-bearer' had become practically universal in the liturgies of East and West. The earliest prayer to Mary dates from the mid third century: *Sub tuum praesidium, sancta Dei Genetrix*, while the doctrinal developments of Ephesus and Chalcedon found an enduring prayerful expression in the Akathist hymn to 'Our Lady the God-bearer and Virgin Mother'. By the end of the 4th century, churches began to be dedicated to Mary and a variety of feasts celebrated in the liturgy. See *Mary: Grace and Hope in Christ*, n 39–40. On a more theological level, see Antonia Antanossova, 'Did Cyril of Alexandria Invent Mariology?', in Maunder, *The Origins of the Cult of the Virgin Mary*, 105–126.

philosophy. There could be no going back to the goddess-worship that Israel had rejected when it encountered the fertility goddesses and the practices of ritual prostitution of its surrounding regions.[29] In New Testament times, Paul's preaching had provoked fierce reaction in Ephesus (Acts 19:23–41). His preaching of the Gospel threatened the cult of Artemis (or Diana as she was called in Rome). Demetrius, the silversmith who had a piece of the roaring trade in statuettes of the goddess, denounced Paul and his associates for undermining the local temple worship—and so for posing a threat to his profits: 'Great is Artemis of the Ephesians!' (Acts 19:34) was the indignant slogan. But the Christian veneration of Mary, emerging as it did from the texts of the New Testament itself, did not regard her as a new temple goddess, nor as female substitute for the deity.[30]

In short, Mary is an icon of the divine, one in whom the light of God shines through; and so, not as an idolic projection of human fabrication. She belonged to a different order of reality. In the unfolding of revelation, she had her own place. It was never doubted that she was a finite, human being. She was an historical woman. Though she, along with everyone else, was redeemed, she occupied a unique position in God's saving design. She stood at the point where the light shifted. As the theology of God developed, so did a theological understanding of Mary and its consequent devotional affectivity find its centre and personal focus.

But with the Reformation in the 16th century, Marian doctrines and devotions became a source of division, despite Luther's keen theological appreciation of Mary and his inspiring commentary on the *Magnificat*. The besetting problem, of course, was what was perceived as devotional excesses taking away from the sole mediation of Christ. Later still, the snag was Catholic ecclesiology as the Magisterium proceeded to define as solemn doctrines of the Immaculate Conception

---

29. See the informative section of George Tavard, *The Thousand Faces of the Virgin Mary* (Collegeville, MN: Liturgical Press, 1996), 221–247: Canaan and Syria had Anath, Astarte and Asherah; the Balylonians venerated Ishtar, while Phrygia had Cybele, the Great Mother; whereas Egypt revered quite a pantheon of female deities (Hathor, Matit, Medfet, Wadjet, and the goddess of learning, Nekhbit, and, above all, Isis.

30. See John Mc Guckin, 'The Early Cult of Mary and Inter-Religious Contexts in the Fifth Century Church', in Maunder, *The Origins of the Cult of the Virgin Mary*, 1–22, for a comprehensive and incisive overview.

(1854) and the Assumption (1950)—which, to the Protestant mind, had no clear scriptural basis. A more theological and ecumenical shift in the Catholic receptivity to the Marian phenomenon occurred in efforts to integrate the mystery of Mary into the life of the Church, as in chapter 8 of the Constitution on the Church, *Lumen Gentium*.[31] Paul VI sought to remove any implication of diminishing the role of Mary soon after the end of Vatican II, and to place Mary in the larger context of grace, Christ and the Church, with his Apostolic Exhortation, *Marialis Cultus* in 1974.[32] John Paul II, intensely Marian in his spirituality (cf. the Marian significance of his motto, *totus tuus*), in his *Redemptoris Mater* (1987),[33] offered a deeply contemplative exposition of the both conciliar teaching in relation to a wide field of biblical data, and voiced the ecumenical significance of the role of Mary for Christian faith. One fruit of this new receptivity was the ARCIC document, *Mary: Grace and Hope in Christ.*

Key Terms in the Marian phenomenon

In this respect, the Marian phenomenon occurs as the matrix of four converging perspectives. Mary is given to faith:

- in her relation to the *dramatis personae*, the Father, Son and Holy Spirit, of God's Trinitarian self-revelation;
- as participating in the paschal enactment in the death and resurrection of Christ;
- as belonging to the sacramental actualisation in the Church throughout history;
- as anticipating the eschatological realisation of God's design.

---

31. The aim was to 'to explain carefully both the role of the Blessed Virgin in the mystery of the Word Incarnate and of the Mystical Body, as well as the duties of the redeemed human race towards the God-bearer, mother of Christ and mother of humanity, especially of the faithful' (*Lumen Gentium*, #54). This more patristic emphasis on the Christological and ecclesial placed Mary in the broader context of Church life and faith (#68-69) as a sign of hope and encouragement for the pilgrim People of God.
32. Paul VI, *Marialis Cultus*, (AAS 66 (1974) 113–168). Note also the preceding documents, the Encyclical Letter, *Christi Matri* (AAS 58 (1966) 745–749), and the Apostolic Exhortation, *Signum Magnum* (AAS 59 (1967) 465:475).
33. John Paul II, *Redemptoris Mater*.

Seven evocative (and irreplaceable, even if equivalent) theological terms interplay within the language of faith: Father, Son, Cross, Resurrection, Spirit, Church, and eschatological fulfilment.[34] These, in turn, can be related to the Johannine 'short formula', 'God is love' (1 Jn 4:8, 16).[35] What is expressed thereby is the conviction that the love of God is the source, form and end of all existence. The revelation of God's self-giving love was the matrix from which the doctrine of the Trinity emerged within the consciousness of the Church. The doctrinal challenge suggested above consisted in articulating as accurately as possible the meaning of the Johannine statement: 'Everyone who loves is born of God and knows God. Whoever does not love does not know God, for God is love' (1 Jn 4:8).[36] It invites an active participation in the revealed mystery with profound epistemological consequences: 'Beloved, let us love one another, because love is from God; everyone who loves is born of God and knows God' (1 Jn 4:7)

Thus, the theological impact of the Marian phenomenon is manifested in the excess of love implied in:

1. the primordial initiative of the *Father*;
2. the self-giving represented in the *Son*;
3. the unconditional love of the *Cross*;
4. the transformative power of the *Resurrection*;
5. the gift of the *Spirit*, communicated throughout history;
6. the historical and sacramental form of the *Church*;
7. the *eschatological* consummation of the divine design.

Each of these seven terms is evocative of the holographic event of God's self-revelation as it saturates Christian consciousness. Each of these seven 'flash points' in the Christian narrative invites faith to reflect how Mary 'shifts the light', so to speak, and embodies the 'transformative summons' that Steiner spoke of. In each case, Mary acts and reveals because she has first received.

---

34. I have chosen this particular order for present purposes, while acknowledging that any of them can be the starting point with a different ordering as a result. I would emphasise, however, that no one of these terms (or its equivalent) can be omitted from any account of Christian faith, without causing a serious distortion.
35. Bernard Sesboüé, 'Le Groupe des Dombes: Marie dans le dessein de Dieu', *Etudes*, 3884, Avril 1998: 513–519.
36. See Kelly, *The Trinity of Love*, 141–173.

Seven Evocative Correlations

Father:

The New Testament's naming of God as *Father* suggests that 'God is love' in an utterly original way.[37] The source of all creation is God's eternal and primordial begetting of divine Word, the only-begotten Son. Through the Son, the Father freely conceives of the whole universe, and calls it into existence. In his Word and Spirit, the Father loves everything into being:[38] 'In this is love, not that we loved God, but that he loved us, and sent his Son to be the atoning sacrifice for our sins' (1 Jn 4:10). From this first divine person comes the initiative more original than any human effort and preceding all created possibilities of responding or believing. In this regard, God's primal love is more original than any original sin. It comes before any consideration of human merit or guilt. God's free grace is determined by no human worth or good work (Ps 139:13-16; Jer 1:4-5; Rom 8:28-30; 2 Tim 1:9)

In relation to God as Father, how is Mary a living icon of God's love? How does the motherhood of Mary affect the Christian understanding of the Fatherhood of God? In the long history of Catholic and Orthodox liturgical and spiritual traditions, an answer is found only on a lived, implicit level. However further articulated, it is ever the case that Mary receives. Through what Catholics have come to call her 'Immaculate Conception', Mary uniquely embodies humanity under the antecedent sway of grace—to be freed from all stain of original sin. The God-ordained destiny of all is eminently expressed in her special giftedness. As Saint Paul exultantly prays,

> Blessed by the God and Father of our Lord Jesus Christ, who has blessed us in Christ with every spiritual blessing in the heavenly places, just as he chose us in Christ before the foundation of the world to be holy and blameless before him in love (Eph 1:3-4).

---

37. See Anthony J Kelly and Francis J. Moloney, *The Experience of God in the Gospel of John* (New York: Paulist, 2003), 389-394.

38. Note, of course, the sheer gifted quality of God's love: it presupposes nothing, so that 'the love of God is ever creating and inpouring the goodness of things' (*amor Dei est creans et infundens bonitatem in rebus*). See Aquinas, *STh* 1, q 20, a 2).

The perverse 'originality' of sin consisted in its power to infect human history with murderous violence and enmity (Gen 4:1–16). To be preserved free from such complicity in evil means that Mary has nothing within her to close her against others. She is uninfected by the bias of evil and pride. She is originally open to the all-inclusive totality of God's saving will. Her vocation is to be a purely generative influence in human history. Grace, God's original and unstinted gift, has destined her to be the New Eve, 'the mother of all the living' (Gen 3:20). In Christian terms, she is the Mother of the whole Christ, head and members.

Though gifted with a singular destiny, she is in no sense divine. Every element of her being is God-given; all her grace has been received. As the Mother of Christ, she is creation at its most generative, 'Blessed among women'. She is 'full of grace' and freed from sin as the chosen associate of the eternally generative Father. Thus, in the fullness of time, she becomes the human Mother of his Son: 'For the Mighty One has done great things for me . . .' (Lk 1:49). Her receptivity to God is the foundation of her gracious relationship to all.

Her receptivity to the Father results in a unique role. To her alone it is given to be the Mother of God, *Theotokos*, the 'God-bearer'. To confess her as the Mother of *God* means to acknowledge her as the human mother of the Word made flesh. A distorted, minimalist view of Mary's motherhood would see her as only the mother of the body or human nature of Christ in the Nestorian sense. But no mother is ever simply a producer of a nature or a body. The physical and generative aspects of motherhood occur within the world of persons. Because motherhood is interpersonal, Mary is personally related to her son, to the person he is, in his radical identity as 'God from God, Light from Light'. The genesis of the universe has needed fifteen billion years. Life has emerged from primitive matter and reaches a luminous peak in human consciousness. The religious searching of Israel's faith in God at work in all things culminates in her consent to be the mother of Jesus. The One who was in the beginning, within the eternal procession of the Son from the Father, now has a new beginning in the fabric and history of the created cosmos. The eternally begotten Son is really brought forth in her. Through her, he is born into the world of creation, subjected to it. 'Born of a woman' (Gal 4:4), he would know poverty, live in surrender to the Father's will, enter into the risk of living for the Kingdom of God – and suffer the consequences. By having this human mother, the divine Son is not posturing in humanity. He is incarnate, enfleshed, born as the divine Word, into the pain, darkness and joy of human existence. In the womb of Mary, the world holds a divine reality within it: the Mother of Jesus is the Mother of God.

In her bringing forth the Christ in the power of the Spirit, Mary receives and reveals—as an icon of the Father. Through her Immaculate Conception she is located in that realm of mercy in which 'God so loved the world' (Jh 3:16). She gives her consent at the Annunciation to be the Mother of 'the holy one' (Lk 1:38). She takes the initiative in visiting Elizabeth and witnesses to the overturning power of God in her *Magnificat*. She brings forth her child and ponders the mysteries of God in her heart (Lk 2:19). Simeon foretells the sword that will pierce her heart (Lk 2:35) if she consent to the transcendent divine purpose to be accomplished through her son. In such ways she is participating in the generative love of the Father. The Father will declare in the moment of the Transfiguration, 'This is my beloved Son, listen to him' (Mk 9:7). This divine declaration is echoed in her command at the marriage feast of Cana: 'Do whatever he tells you' (Jn 2:5).[39] Her radical surrender to the self-giving love of God will lead her finally to the Cross. There she stands with the Beloved Disciple. Now that the 'hour' of Jesus has come, he gives his disciple to his Mother, and presents her, in turn, to him (Jn 19:25–27).[40] Suggesting her mediating role amongst the earliest followers and blood relatives of Jesus, Luke locates in the community awaiting the outpouring of the Spirit (Acts 1:14). The Holy Spirit who will come from above onto the early Church is the same Spirit that came upon her to enable her to conceive Jesus at the beginning of his human life.

These luminous New Testament perspectives bring Mary into focus as the woman on whom the play of light shifts and intensifies. A light not of this world makes this woman an icon of the generative, life-giving love of the Father. For all the generations that call her blessed, and hear the words of Jesus, 'Behold, your mother' (Jn 20:27) and take her to themselves,[41] she expresses in a unique manner the tenderness of God, and invitation to 'the perfect love that casts out fear' (1 Jn 4:18). Just as the Father has given what is most intimately his own for the salvation of the world, she has entered into such unreserved self-

---

39. Kelly and Moloney, *The Experience of Gog*, 69–70.
40. Kelly and Moloney, *The Experience of God*, 364–368.
41. Kelly and Moloney, *The Experience of God*, 365–366.

giving. She brings into the world the One whom the Father eternally begets. In time and place, she gives what the Father has given and in the way that God gives, to offer this Son of the Father and her child for the world's salvation: 'God's love was revealed among us in this way. God sent his only Son into the world that we might live through him' (1 Jn 4:9). Thus, Mary figures in the drama of the divine self-giving love intent on bringing life to the world.

Mary's maternal love is the historical human manifestation of the Father's generative love. She is not an idol fabricated by human projections, but a woman in whom the Light shines through. As an icon of the Father in this way, she subverts the religious imagination that would see the ultimate origin in rigidly masculine terms. When the generative, self-giving love of the Father is disclosed in history through the love of this mother, there are consequences. In the interactions of faith and culture, the whole play of human language and symbolism must be deployed in expressing the infinities of God's life and love. She is 'perfect' as 'your Heavenly Father' is (Matt 5:48; Lk 6:36). No particular invocation of God, even under the name of 'Father', can be so absolutised as to curtail the play of the expressiveness of faith and human experience. The name of God who lives in unapproachable light is hallowed neither by dead metaphors, nor by jaded ideologies. The language of faith must be restlessly imaginative. In the current critical task of exploring the meaning of God as Father,[42] theology finds a resource, at once simple and evocative: the motherhood of Mary is a symbol of the Fatherhood of God.

Son:

In the invocation of Christ as the *Son*, the affirmation, 'God is love', resonates as an expression of God's unique self-utterance and self-giving. The incarnation in all its aspects is the climactic divine self-involvement in creation. God does not simply intervene by doing something *for* us—'for us and our salvation'—but becomes personally someone *with* us in the sphere of creation. Christ is *Emmanuel*, 'God-with-us' (Matt 1:23). The Word is made flesh (Jn 1:14). The generative love that is the source of all creation gives into the flesh of our existence its most intimate self-expression: 'This is my beloved Son: hear him!' (Mk 9:7).

---

42. Anthony J Kelly, '"Come to the Father": A Theology of the Fatherhood of God', in *The Australasian Catholic Record* lxxvii/3 (July 1999): 281–291.

The magi in the Gospel of Matthew (Matt 2:11) and the shepherds in that of Luke (Lk 2:16) find Jesus with his mother. And as the Mother of Jesus she embodies the self-giving character of God's love. Yet she gives because she has first received. As the first of the redeemed, she receives all from her Son, for the Word is given into the faith and flesh of her existence. In this receptivity– for apart from him, she, like all believers, can do nothing (Jn 15:5) – she is drawn into the most intimate association with her Son's mission. The Father's 'listen to him!' (*Cf* Mk 9:7) echoes in her instruction to the servants at Cana, 'Do whatever he tells you' (Jn 2:5). The words of Jesus are verified in her: 'My Father is glorified by this, that you bear much fruit and become my disciples' (John 15:8). She indeed bears 'much fruit'. She becomes the Mother of Christ, and the mother of all the faithful. Jesus on the cross instructs her, 'Woman, behold, your son!' (Jn 19:26). The 'son' here is the Beloved Disciple, the embodiment of immediate and unreserved faith. She is now not simply his sister in the new family of God, but his mother: 'Behold, your Mother' (Jn 20:27).

Cross:
The revelation that 'God is love' cannot be separated from the dramatic event of the *Cross*. God's love is disclosed as unconditional and without reserve. It keeps on being love even when exposed to the deepest darkness of the world's evil. At the point where human malice is most manifest in crucifying the Son, the love that God is, keeps on being love as limitless mercy: 'Father, forgive them for they do not know what they are doing' (Lk 23:34). Love at once unmasks and subverts the desperate violence of the loveless.[43]

Here, too, Mary gives as she has received. Greeted by Gabriel as the woman uniquely favoured by God (Lk 1:28, 30), she follows her Son in his mission, and suffers the piercing of soul that Simeon foretold (Lk 2:35). She has been given the Beloved Disciple by the dying Jesus (Jn 20:26). On her, and on this disciple, amongst those gathered at the foot of the cross as representatives of the new community of faith, the Spirit of Jesus has been given: 'Then he bowed his head and handed over the Spirit' (Jn 19:30). A new community of Christ-like selfless love has been born. It must stand against the violently idolatrous self-promotion of this world and its 'ruler' (Jn 14:30; 16:11), by witnessing to another form of community and life.

---

43. On this theme, following the thought of René Girard, Gil Bailie, *Violence Unveiled. Humanity at the Crossroads* (New York: Crossroad, 1997).

In that community of faith, Mary is invoked as the Mother of Mercy. She represents the gentle, ever-persistent presence of the Reign of God, that other kingdom that owes nothing to the inhuman rule of violence and hatred. When challenged by Pilate, Jesus had answered, "My kingdom is not from here . . . For this was I born, and for this I came into the world, to testify to the truth. Everyone who belongs to the truth listens to my voice' (Jn 19:36–37). Jesus' refers to the realm opposed to the murderous self-justifications of power and pride. Pilate's unease is evident in his response, 'What is truth?' (Jn 19:38). The self-glorifying power of the world relegates the kingdom of the true God to the unreal. The 'real world' is constructed on the self-serving ambitions of ruthless power. Its political vocabulary dare not include words such as compassion, forgiveness, humility, obedience to God, self-sacrificing love. The Beatitudes leave it tongue-tied. It has no time for such 'useless'—and dangerous—notions.

But Mary belongs to the truth and has heard its voice. There are those who pray to her, 'Holy Mary, Mother of God, pray for us sinners, now and at the hour of our death.' Their prayer arises from an awareness of the seductive power of evil and the fragility of human freedom. In such a world, love is a scarce resource. If it exists, it is a pact amongst those who in effect reject others outside their circle. But to love as God loves, is to love without conditions or calculations. It is to be vulnerable—in a love that finds its source, support and true measure only in God. In this respect, Mary witnesses to the truth of the love revealed in her Son. By standing before the stark truth of the Cross, she stands against the loveless lie that drives a world of self-enclosure and the exclusion of the powerless. To the degree a culture is permeated by the seven deadly sins,[44] she is something of a threat. Her prayer expresses praise of the God who scatters 'the proud in the thoughts of their hearts'. For her, God is the One who brings down 'the powerful from their thrones' (Lk 1:51–52). In all these ways, Mary at the foot of the cross is a subversive presence.[45]

Resurrection:
Only in the light of her Son's resurrection is Mary known to faith. 'God is love' in a divinely transformative event. Though love is never

---

44. Traditionally listed as pride, covetousness, lust, anger, gluttony, envy and sloth.
45. See René Coste, *The Magnificat. The Revolution of God* (Quezon City: Claretian Publications, 1987).

reduced to the level of worldly power, it is not ineffective. It is not defeated by the powers that crucified Jesus. Love has raised him from the tomb to be the form and source of the life in a new creation. Lifted up from the earth, the crucified Son draws all to himself (Jn 11:52; 12:32). He is the ultimate embodiment of the 'love that bears all things, believes all things, hopes all things, endures all things' (1 Cor 13:4–8).

How does the resurrection affect our perception of Mary? Paul wrote to his Corinthian audience: 'Now if Christ is proclaimed as raised from the dead, how can some of you say there is no resurrection from the dead? If there is no resurrection from the dead, then Christ has not been raised, then our proclamation has been in vain and your faith has been in vain' (1 Cor 15:12–15). By celebrating Mary's assumption into heaven, faith in the resurrection of the Lord finds a correlative symbol. The power of the resurrection has flowed into the existence of this pre-eminent believer, to transform her whole being and to perfect her mission. In terms of Paul's indirect description of risen existence (1 Cor 15:42–58), Mary is no longer subject to the rule of death, nor to the dishonour inevitable in the realm of worldly glory, nor to the weakness that worldly power consigns it. Her transformed existence is no long enclosed in the spiritless materialism of a world undisturbed by the creative imagination of God's Spirit. In her union with her Son, 'the resurrection and the life' (Jn 11:25), she exemplifies faith in its radical, defiant and universal hope: 'If for this life only we have hoped in Christ, we are of all people most to be pitied. But in fact Christ has been raised from the dead, the first fruits of those who have died' (1 Cor 15:19).

In the power of her Son's resurrection, Mary now lives and acts: 'Surely, from now on, all the generations will call me blessed' (Lk 1:48). God is not the God of the dead, but of the living (Mt 22:32). She lives, acts, and continues to act, from the heart of God's transforming love through intercessory prayer and compassionate involvement in the great travail of creation (Rom 8:22). Invoked as Our Lady Help of Christians, as the Mother of Mercy and of Grace, as the Mother of Perpetual Help—indeed, in all the invocations of the Litany of Loreto—she is related to all in the communion of saints. She anchors faith, inspires hope, and exemplifies the 'love [that] never ends' (1 Cor 13:8). Assumed into heaven, she collaborates with the New Adam as the New Eve in a maternal relationship with all believers.

Mary of Nazareth is the name of an historical person. Yet history has no record of her except through the documents of faith, above all the Gospels of the New Testament, and in what has been written in the hearts of believers through the ages. She is known to faith through its awareness of the universal transformation anticipated in the resurrection of her Son. She stands where the light has shifted in human hope; where the power of death and evil has been overcome.

Spirit:
'God is love' by communicating the gift of the *Spirit* to every age. The love that originated in the Father, that is incarnate in the life, death and resurrection of the Son, is breathed into history as a liberating life-force. The Breath of God is the divine atmosphere invigorating the life of believers in every time and place. In the Spirit, 'the Lord and giver of life', Christ was conceived, the Church brought into being, and all creation moves in a new energy toward its fulfilment (Rom 8:26).

How is Mary linked to this gift of the Spirit? Through the Spirit, the Father begets the Son in eternity. Through the Spirit acting in Virgin Mary, the Father begets his only Son in time. In the words of Gabriel, 'The Holy Spirit will come upon you, and the power of the Most High will overshadow you' (Lk 1:35). God's self-giving love is not restricted or conditioned by what creation can produce in terms of human reproduction or generation. Her virginal maternity discloses the incalculable initiative of the Spirit in regard to all the children of God, 'who were born, not of blood or the will of the flesh or the will of man, but of God' (Jn 1:13). In confessing her precisely as the *Virgin* Mary, faith acts in adoration of the imaginative power of God to bring forth the new. It culminates in the reality of God-with-us— definitively in the Word made flesh, derivatively in everyone who 'is born of the Spirit' (Jn 3:8). Where the Breath of the Spirit plays, it transforms all it touches, including this Jewish woman, Mariam. She receives the Spirit, yet acts in the power of this divine Gift, for she has been chosen to be the created human collaborator in the incarnation itself. Her virginal maternity is a unique 'manifestation of the Spirit for the common good' (1 Cor 12:7). By the power of the Spirit, Jesus is conceived, to be born of the Virgin Mary. Under the inspiration of the Spirit, faith defines her being: she is pure receptivity to the Spirit, pure attention to the Word, pure adoration of the Father: 'My soul magnifies the Lord . . .' (Lk 1:40). She is defined in no other way, by no other relationship—neither by a human partner, nor by social expectations, nor by human ambition, nor even by the common religious notions of her time or ours. What determines her existence is solely what God can be and what God can do. She is the woman who most intimately knows that 'for God nothing is impossible' (Lk 1:37). Yet, in her Spirit-formed existence, divine freedom collaborates communicates with a created freedom. Divine love calls forth a human love to be its partner in the world's transformation.[46]

In the horizon that refuses to impose any limits on the Spirit and the divine imagination, the Blessed Virgin Mary is invoked in the faith of the Church. In this she stands at the point where the new covenant promised by the prophets of Israel is realised: 'This is the covenant which I will make with the house of Israel after those days, says the Lord: I will put my law within them, and I will write it upon their hearts; and I will be their God, and they shall be my people' (Jer 31:33. *Cf* also, Ezek 36:25–28).

Her virginal maternity has its meaning only within the universe of grace. At this point, faith must learn its own reserve. There is no place for any form of theological voyeurism. All efforts to reduce God's 'impossible ways' to the humanly familiar are in vain. Her identity is disclosed only in the light of the resurrection of her Son and in the consequent outpouring of the Spirit. She is named only in the vocabulary of a new language speaking, with defiant hope, of the world's transformation in Christ. She belongs to the realm where love is revealed as the power at work to make all things new.

When faith turns to Mary, it recognises her unique role in God's self-communication to the world. The Spirit, active in all creation and throughout the 'all generations', brings the world and its history to a unique point of freedom in this woman. She consents on behalf of creation to receive into itself the mystery from which all existence derives. In her free consent to what God is to bring about, she is the world's overture to the power of the Holy Spirit. All the faithfulness of generations before her and after her, all their waiting on God and their yielding to the Spirit, are condensed in her act of self-surrender: 'Be it done unto me according to your Word' (Lk 1:38).

---

46. See Anthony J Kelly, *An Expanding Theology. Faith in a World of Connections* (Sydney: EJ Dwyer, 1993), 171–172.

In this 'Virgin Daughter of Sion', all the hopes and faith of her people are condensed. Elizabeth, summing up the Old Testament praise of the faithful, proclaims, 'Blessed is she who believed that there would be a fulfilment of what was spoken to her by the Lord' (Lk 1:45). She stands both at the culminating point of the past history of divine promises, and at the beginning of their unheard-of fulfilment. Through her unconditional yielding to what the Spirit alone can accomplish, the Word adored in her faith is conceived in her womb. Henceforth, her whole life and destiny are bound up with her Son and his mission. The virginal motherhood of Mary expresses two essential and related aspects of divine action. First, the Holy Spirit is not reducible to any created power; and, secondly, God acts within the powers and freedom of creation. The incarnation of the eternal Word comes about from beyond, and yet it occurs from within the realm of creation through human cooperation. Precisely because the divine power so transcends the created order, it can work so intimately within to it. Though the Son is incarnate by the power of the Spirit, he is still truly 'born of the Virgin Mary'.

Church:
'God is love' looks to an historical and identifiable embodiment from generation to generation in the *Church*. In the pilgrim, sacramental reality of Church, the saving mystery is celebrated and offered to the world. As it mediates Christ to the world, the ecclesial community is an open circle. It lives from, and witnesses to, the grace at work in all lives. It can be considered as that part of world which has woken to the superabundance of God's love.

Standing at the foot of the cross, Mary stands at the foundation of the Church. In the revelatory event of the Cross the figures of the Eve, Church, Mary and Christian discipleship interweave. The first woman was taken from Adam's 'rib' (Gen 2:22, *pleura* LXX) and became the mother of all the living (Gen 3:20). So, too, is Mary in the new community of the Church is the mother of all who receive the gift of eternal life from the water and blood flowing from the pierced side (again, *pleura*, literally 'rib') of the Crucified Jesus (Jn 19:34), and from the Spirit he breathes forth (Jn 19:30, 20:22, *Cf* 1 Jn 5:8). In this Johannine perspective, Mary is both the archetype and first realization of the Church.[47] Her unconditional Yes to the design

---

47. *Mary: Grace and Hope in Christ*, n 27.

of God takes her to the Cross, and to her place in the community of the disciples, as they await the outpouring of the Spirit that had so possessed her from the beginning (Acts 1:18). She is a personal symbol of the Church's corporate identity.

Mary is a luminous presence in the 'cloud of witnesses' (Heb 12:1) permeating the atmosphere of faith, a focal presence in the great 'communion of saints' gathered in praising he God of all gifts (*Cf* Rev 6:9–11; 7; 8:3–4). In her, the Church finds its paradigm and exemplar of what it is called to be, 'So that she may be holy and without blemish' (*Cf* Eph 5:25–27). In union with the Mother of the Redeemer, 'Mother Church' contends with the antagonistic powers of the world. The history of evil, of the Antichrist, contends with 'a great portent in the heaven: a woman clothed with the sun, with the moon under her feet, and on her head a crown of twelve stars. She is pregnant and crying out in birth-pangs in the agony of giving birth' (Rev 12:1–2). A new creation is being born.

Despite the jumbled ambiguity of the actual community of saints and sinners, the Church possesses an unfailing generative holiness: 'Holy Mother Church'. Like Mary, and in union with her, the Church is holy only because God is holy, because the Body of Christ is holy, and because the all-creative Spirit is holy. In the depths of its life, the Church inhales the Holy Spirit. Such holiness does not fail. The inexhaustible source of the Church's holiness is already realised in Mary and the 'holy ones', the saints and the great company of the apostles, martyrs and faithful witnesses in every age. Their influence precedes and accompanies, sustains and blesses the often sorry efforts of the Church in any era.

In all that she has received, in all that she is now for us, Mary is the living, acting embodiment of the God-given holiness of the Church. Whatever the sins of us Christians, individual, political or social, whatever the failings of our institutional leaders, it is only in the Church that we first met Christ, heard the Gospel and celebrated the Eucharist. Mary invites us in every age, even in the face of scandals of all kinds, to be open to the whole reality of the Church. It is always a temptation to become so censoriously fixated in some distorted fragment of the ecclesiastical reality that the holiness of the Church drops out of consideration. Scandal can be a convenient excuse for not being involved in the flesh-and-blood history of faith– with all its demands, risks and ambiguities—by hiding behind our own projections of unliveable excellence. It is possible to become all too anorexic in our appreciation of the Body of Christ in history. The temptation is to invent a self-justifying private religious 'purity', isolated from, and even against, the corporate, pilgrim existence as the Church. A Marian sense of the Church helps faith to keep a sense of proportion. Its confession of the 'holy Church' confronts believers with the grace of God far more humanly incarnate in our midst than any kind of precious, irritated moralism can perceive. Mary is not a compensation for a lack of holiness, but a living invitation to conversion, for she already embodies the holiness to which are called.

Eternal Life:

Finally, 'God is love' as gathering believers through Christ and the Spirit into 'the life of the world to come'. Love is at work to bring creation to its fulfilment. The creative source of all that is has made time for the emergence of the world and for the enactment of the whole drama of human freedom. The self-giving love of God is pulsing in every moment of the world's history. It has been active in every event and human agent. It has guided the complex dynamics of this emerging cosmos. All along, God's love has been intent on that final moment of fulfilment in order 'that God may be all in all' (1 Cor 15:28). God is love, therefore, as the first and last word on the divine destiny of all creation, moving towards its final consummation and unveiling. Christ is risen, and 'behold, the new has come' (2 Cor 5:17).

Ambrose of Milan sums up the cosmic scope of what has taken place: 'In Christ's resurrection the world arose. In Christ's resurrection, the heavens arose; in Christ's resurrection the earth itself arose.'[48] In this eschatological perspective, Mary's Assumption is the realisation of her full-bodied possession of eternal life. Here, as in all else, Mary receives from Christ. In anticipation of this universal transformation, Mary, 'assumed body and soul into heaven', is already taken up into the glory of Christ. As with all the grace of Mary, the Assumption is not an exclusively Marian privilege, but the anticipation of transfigured creation and the destiny of the Spirit-charged world.[49] She is the paradigm instance of creation surrendered to the God

---

48. *De excessu fratris sui*, bk 1. *PL* 16, 1354.
49. See Karl Rahner, 'The Interpretation of the Dogma of the Assumption', in *Theological Investigations I*, translated by C Ernst (London: Darton, Longman and Todd, 1961), 215–227.

who transforms all in Christ. Both the generativity and the destiny of God's creation are revealed in her for, as the Advent antiphon has it, "the earth has been opened to bud forth the Saviour".

The seer of the Apocalypse invites faith into the vision of 'the holy city, the new Jerusalem, coming down out of heaven from God, prepared as a bride adorned for her husband' (Rev 21:1–3). As the Spirit descended on Mary to make her the Mother of Christ and Mother of the Church, and as she is assumed into glory, the great cosmic marriage is begun. The Spirit has formed in her the particular beauty of creation in the sight of God. In her consent to be the Mother of Christ, history has reached its age of consent—in surrender to the transcendent love for which it was destined (*Cf* Eph 5:21-33; Rev 21:9). Out of such a union, the whole Christ of a transfigured creation is born.

Conclusion

By reflecting briefly on seven evocative and irreplaceable terms (*Father, Son Cross, Resurrection, Spirit, Church and eternal life*), we have attempted evoke something of the 'saturated' character of Mary's presence to the Church. In the matrix of this manifold phenomenon, we have suggested something of the meaning of Marian doctrines and symbols guided by the most fundamental of all Christian affirmations, 'God is Love'. While the focus of Christian hope is on Christ's death and resurrection, in Mary it has both a *reprise* and 're-presentation' in anticipation of what is to come. In her, hope celebrates the grace of God, given, received, and working its transformation. In their communion with Mary, Christians become more deeply receptive to the sweep and scope of the unfolding of mystery of mercy 'from age to age to those who revere him' (Lk 1:50).

Mary and the Heart

It seems to many that the ozone layer of the old secular beliefs and Enlightenment certitudes has been massively holed. Under the sun of a new consciousness the violent ways of our planetary humanity have been exposed. Faced with the troubles of regions such the Middle East, Africa, the Ukraine and Korea, Western nations hesitate between playing the parts of John Wayne or Mother Teresa. Whether we look within our own country or beyond it, the recognition of the number of victims seems to increase exponentially. What is the meaning of this new conscience? What is breaking out?

History suggests that we seldom suspect what great changes we are living through. But something is clear: the once-acceptable levels of force employed for the preservation of state or empire or the revolution or the world order—or even for the defence of 'humanity' itself—seem to have gone beyond all human proportion.

Over a hundred years ago, the magnificently intelligent but increasingly mad Nietzsche wrote a perceptive indictment of Christianity:

> I condemn Christianity. I raise against the Christian church the most terrible of all accusations that any accuser ever uttered . . . The Christian church has left nothing untouched by its corruption . . . The 'equality of souls' before God, this falsehood, this *pretext* for the rancor of all the base-minded, this explosive of a concept that eventually became revolution, modern idea, and the principle of decline of the whole order of society—is *Christian* dynamite.[1]

---

1. *The Portable Nietzsche*, edited and translated by Walter Kaufmann (New York: Penguin, 1968), 655.

By its preaching of the beatitudes, and Christ's command to love our suffering neighbour, by calling attention to the victims of our history united in the mystery of the Cross, Christianity is condemned by its brilliant crazed antagonist as 'siding with all that is weak and base . . . We are deprived of strength when we feel pity . . . Some have dared call pity a virtue (in every noble ethic it is considered a weakness. And as if that were not enough, it has been made *the* virtue, the basis and source of all virtues.'[2] Against such a conscience, Nietzsche exalted the will to power, the pride of the super-man; and so prepared the way for what even for him would have been a nightmare—the Nazi Reich.

Just note how such a world-view is opposed to the language of the *Magnificat*: 'My soul glorifies the Lord, my spirit rejoices in God my saviour; he looks on his servant in her lowliness; henceforth all generations will call me blessed.' But it would not be so for Nietzsche's 'superman'. This young Jewish woman is the antithesis of everything it stands for. Her God ' . . . puts forth his arm in strength, and scatters the proud hearted. He casts the mighty from their thrones and raises the lowly.' Whose prediction, Nietzsche's or Mary's, has been more obviously fulfilled? Therein lies the crisis of our day. Will this God 'fill the starving with good things and send the rich away empty'? What if our world does not notice the starving? What if the void in the lives of these 'proud-hearted' and 'mighty' ones should unleash ever more demonic efforts to fill their emptiness with more victims? Does the faith of Israel end in the gas-chamber and ovens of Auschwitz, or does Miriam, this daughter of Israel, speak more truly: 'He protects Israel his servant, remembering his mercy, the mercy promised to our fathers, to Abraham and his seed forever'. History continues to vacillate at the point of crisis. On the one side, there are the idols of race, greed and power driven by the demons of the seven deadly sins, with an imagination fixed on self-promotion, revenge, and haunted with the dread of death. On the other side, there is another realm of life, and another language spoken by this woman: Praise and humility, a joyful confidence in the God of marvellous impossibilities, a universal hope for divine mercy, the role of the God's servant in the world . . . How can the New Eve take us, beyond Adam's scapegoating of the old Eve, beyond her blaming the serpent, beyond the serpent's

---

2. *The Portable Nietzsche*, 572.

complaint against God, beyond Cain's murderous envy of Abel (for the first death the Bible records is a murder), and into the life of a new humanity?

Admittedly, it is possible that a self-consciously respectable religion can disdain the figure of Mary and popular devotion in places of pilgrimages and special shrines dedicated to her honour. Theology can be coy: Can it be so cowed by the truculence Nietzsche's denunciation of Christianity that becomes tongue-tied and embarrassed on the subject of Mary?

In the assurance of faith, Christians must be only to be rational, but intelligent; not only intelligent but deeply intelligent—in recognising that 'The heart has reasons which reason itself does not know' (Pascal).

It is beyond dispute that a development has occurred in the Church's understanding of Mary; and that it needs to continue. Let me take you back to one key component in that developing understanding as we find it in John's Gospel. Here, the Cross is the moment of culminating hour of divine revelation. When that hour strikes in God's timing of events, all are drawn to the crucified Son (Jn 12:32), and the scattered children of God are gathered into one (Jn 11:52–53), to realise that Jesus is indeed the bearer of the divine name, 'I am he' (Jn 8:27). At that hour, Jesus commends his Mother and his Beloved Disciple to each other's keeping: 'Woman, behold, your son!' and, 'Behold, your Mother' (Jn 19:26–27). The Gospel reports that 'from that hour, the disciple took her to his own home' (v 27b). Current biblical research[3] suggests that 'from' (*apo* followed by the genitive case) carries the associated meaning of 'because of' that hour. Because of Jesus' being lifted up on the cross, his Mother and his disciple become one. The Beloved Disciple had been characterised by a special intimacy with Jesus (13:23) and a special insight into the water and blood flowing from pierced side of the Crucified (19:34–36). He directs the community of faith to see the scriptures fulfilled in what has taken place—as 'they look on him whom they have pierced'. His faith in the resurrection is especially gifted, for it relies on no other witness, not even the scriptures themselves (20:8). And because of his faith and witness he has a continuing special vocation in the

---

3. See for example Frank Moloney, *Gospel of John* (Collegeville, MN: Michael Glazier, 2005), 503–504.

Christian community as it reads the Gospel (21:20–24). He appears to embody the deepest and most faith-filled awareness of the Church in its recollection of its central mystery.

To that figure, Mary has been given, not as a sister in faith, but as his Mother; and so, he receives her as a gift into the intimacy of his life. It seems to me, then, that maternal presence of Mary is most registered where faith is most alive to the meaning of the Word, incarnate, crucified and risen. Is not this the deepest source of a developing understanding of Mary and of deeper receptivity to her role and witness? Mary herself embodies the meaning of faith, to mediate its deepest meaning to the community that acknowledges its origins in the witness of the Beloved disciple. It is a continuing dynamic, for that witness continues in history. In its feel for the fullness of Christ, new things, new aspects of the mystery emerge. Through her we are led to something more original than original sin, the immaculate conception of humanity realised in her—the original grace at work in creation before the cultures of violence clamped our history into its pride, envy and murderous exclusion of the other.

In a larger context, let us visit a significant incident in the writings of Luke who has written more about Mary than any of the New Testament writers. The passage that concerns us is found in Acts 8:26–40. Here the main character is Philip. Interestingly, the last glimpse we have of Philip in John's Gospel is when he said to Jesus, 'Lord, show us the Father and we shall be satisfied' (Jn 14:8). The Lord proceeds to bring his disciple back to earth: 'Have I been with you all this time, Philip, and you still do not know me? Whoever has seen me, has seen the Father. How can you say, 'Show us the Father'? (v 9). The Father—who 'judges no one' (Jn 5:22)—is revealed only in his love for the world, evidenced in the gift of his only Son. Philip has been looking up to heaven for some momentous vision, when all the time the one true God was being revealed in the violent darkness of the world in which the disciples lived. Let us not forget that is where Mary, too, had found him, or, more correctly, God had found her.

In the incident recorded in Acts, it is Philip's turn to bring someone else down to earth. He is on a missionary journey on the desert road between Jerusalem and Gaza. He is inspired to link up with the entourage of a high-ranking official in the Ethiopian court of Queen Candace, who happens to be returning from a pilgrimage to Jerusalem. Approaching the great man's chariot, Philip hears him reading a passage dealing with the Suffering Servant in Isaiah: 'Like a sheep he was led to the slaughter,/ and a like a lamb silent before its shearers,/ he does not open his mouth./ In his humiliation, justice was denied him./ Who can describe his generation?/ For his life is taken away from the earth' (*Cf* Acts 8:32; Isa 53:7–8). Philip somewhat forwardly asks whether His Excellency understands what he is reading. 'How can I', he replies, 'unless there is someone to guide me'? (v 31). So it happens that Philip is invited to come in and sit beside him on that bumpy desert road, and is further asked to solve the riddle of that past defenceless figure who has so innocently suffered. Isaiah wrote of one from whom people recoiled in horror: 'He was despised, and we held him of no account' (v. 3). But despite the mob violence suffered by this innocent one, there was a wondrous glimmering of something else: 'Surely he has borne our iniquities and carried our diseases; yet we accounted stricken, cut down by God, and afflicted. But he wounded for our transgressions, crushed for our iniquities, upon him was the punishment that made us whole, and by his bruises we are healed' (vv 4–5). So, for Philip, quite a bit of explaining to do. How could this defenceless figure subject to the violence of others be a source of healing for them? The royal official in good exegetical style, puts a question to Philip: 'About whom, may I ask, does the Prophet say this, about himself or about someone else?' (Acts 8:34). It appears that Philip was up to the task: 'starting with this scripture, he proclaimed to him the good news about Jesus' (v 35). So much so, indeed, that as they came to an oasis on that hot track the official volunteered for baptism. And it was done. Philip went off in the power of the Spirit, and the court official went on his way rejoicing (v 39).

What had he discovered? What gave this new sense of joy? At the risk of jumbling scriptural references, but still to give the simplest and truest answer, Philip has led the official to see what Jesus had made him see—the reality of the Father; and in the process, to find himself. Both aspects of this enlightenment happened through the word of the Cross, God revealed in the defencelessness and power of utter love. In that crucified one the all-inclusive and all-disarming mystery of the Father, and the earthly form of the eternal life of our true humanity is revealed. What we most value is not at the mercy of what we dread. What we most hope for is at the mercy of—Mercy itelf!. In the light of that cross, humanity is offered its culminating opportunity to go beyond the violent ever-shrinking economy of envy, and all the self-promoting nonsense of worldly glory, to enter a superabundant economy of grace in which the first shall be last, and the last first, and the most unrecognised and defenceless are closest to God.

Those whom their faith enables to inhale the atmosphere of that other world, to feel the morning freshness of the resurrection, to breathe the free air of the beatitudes in a readiness to love their neighbour and even their enemies, find in Mary the inspiration and 'perpetual help' necessary for living the Christ-life.

So much of culture is imitation; and so much of that imitation consists in wanting what others want. The envious desire to be like others coveting their power, their fame, their possessions, their security, their beauty, their independence. By being drawn into such patterns of cultural imitation—and modern advertising knows a lot about this – we make the idols that have demanded so much human sacrifice throughout history. What would happen if we opened ourselves to another desire and another imagination, to take seriously the prayer we have been given to say, '*Our* Father, hallowed by *thy* name, *thy* kingdom come, *thy* will be done, on earth and it is in heaven'? It is a struggle; and the world's history has been long and dark. The words of John at the end of his letter to a community in which we can recognise ourselves have a piercing relevance: 'Little children, keep yourselves from idols' (1 Jn 4:21).

The influence of Mary in the life of faith works chiefly to inspire us to enter this other world of desire. All the references to her scattered through the Gospels tell something of her desire. Listen to her *Fiat* at the Annunciation, to the Magnificat. Consider how she pondered the mystery in her heart; and her unquestioning faith at Cana when her final words recorded in the Gospel of the Word are 'Do whatever he tells you' (Jn 2:5)—with the result that the water is changed into wine, a sign of a world transformed by his coming. Look at her at the foot of the cross and waiting with the disciples at the first Pentecost. All these references form a certain *Gestalt*. She is, in body and heart, given over to that transforming grace which is at once a judgment on the world and the advent of its salvation. Her own grace within this universal grace is articulated in the solemn Marian doctrines of the Church: her Immaculate Conception, Divine Maternity, and Assumption into heaven; and, less formally, expressed in that procession of feasts that bring into Christian consciousness her exemplary role in and for the

Church as the words of her Son continue to resonate in Christian lives from generation to generation: 'Woman, behold, your son!'; 'Behold, your Mother!'. If Jesus is the desire and imagination of God incarnate among us, Mary embodies, in her womb and in her heart, a desire conformed to his desire; and an imagination living from her Son's way of imagining his Father and the coming Kingdom. The desire of the world has been confronted by Jesus' example and new commandment: 'For I have set you an example, that you should do as I have done to you' (Jn 13:15).

While Church teaching is somewhat nervous about the ambiguities of invoking her as the Mediatrix of all graces lest it obscure the role of Christ the Mediator, it is useful to set her mediation in the broadest context. To the imagination of Catholic faith, all the founding figures of our history from Adam and Eve and Abel, Abraham and Moses, the Prophets, the Apostles, and the great saints and martyrs right down to our own time, mediate something of the meaning of God's revelation to us. Each of these, and many more besides, means the world to us in their respective ways.

This to say that in the service of the mediation of the grace of Our Lord Jesus Christ, the love of God and the fellowship of the Holy Spirit, each of these figures, each of these presences in the universe of grace, embodies, incarnates, mediates that grace in some way. For example, in the communion of saints, Peter mediates the pastoral role of unifying authority in the Church. Paul embodies the realities of grace, freedom and conversion. John, Beloved Disciple or not, incarnates the central mystery of God's love.

In the midst of all these mediations, Mary typically mediates the totality of the Church's meaning as a communion in Christ, since she is the Mother of all. As well, she mediates the basic function of its mission, to bring forth the whole Christ in the world, since she is the Mother of the Redeemer himself. In the family of God she is essentially related to us, to share what she herself has so eminently received. She brings home to us, in the deepest recesses of our feelings and imagination, the tender mercies of our God.

But all such mediations, hers and that of all the saints, serve the mission of the unique mediator. If you like, each one is an incarnation of meaning in the history of the Incarnation of the Word. Without such mediations, the imagination of the Church would be humanly incomplete. Admittedly, in this approach, we are using the term 'mediation' in a more general philosophical sense, compared to the theologically saturated manner it is employed in formal Catholic teaching. Still, this broader, more open-ended sense makes some useful space when ecumenical dialogue is trying to find in Mary, not a sign of contradiction, but a gracious symbol of unity.

What then does Mary mediate in her role in the economy of grace and in the imagination of that grace in community of faith? Granting the emphasis of Vatican II, one can hardly deny that Mary incarnates the holiness and creativity of the Church itself. Within the Church, she is a symbol *for* the Church, the presence of what the Church is destined to be. But there is a deeper level. As *Theotokos*, as the God-bearer, as the Mother of God, Mary is a unique mediator of the meaning of the trinitarian love of God. In giving birth to her Son, she is an icon of the Father. As the first of believers, as the one most receptive in heart an7d body to the reality of Christ, she is an icon of the Son. And of course, possessed by the Spirit, and given to the Church in the person of the Beloved Disciple, she is an icon of the ever fruitful love of the Spirit.

We could leave it there; but the trouble is that we do not tend to stay *there*, in complete and unreserved surrender to the God of self-giving love at work in our lives and through all the universe. The heart of stone can replace the heart of flesh. We can find ourselves conforming to the heartless, self-promoting, covetous dynamics of our world, so to be in continual danger of fabricating a god to serve our own little kingdoms, by turning the God of our Lord Jesus Christ into some kind of larger angel summoned forth from time to time to help us get our way. So, we begin to absolutise our unredeemed desires to possess, to consume, to exclude, to own, to centre the universe in ourselves. A murderous moralism soon begins to imagine God condemning the inhabitants of the evil empire, or of 'the axis of evil' in terms of the most unreformed system of justice. We all assist by keeping 'a little list', with its meticulous account of merits, and the range of possible punishments to fit the crime. To the degree the imagination of faith is infested with vengeful fantasies, the world becomes more harsh, more doomed; and there is less time and less energy to care for those about whom no one cares—the old, the sick, the poor, the unfortunate, the disgraced, the foreigner, the stranger at the door . . . We human beings cling to the absolutes that guarantee our security from all such threats, the idols of race, of political power, of national security, of greed, of a religion that never knew what mercy meant.

Blasphemous, of course. 'Little children, keep yourself from idols' (1 Jn 4:21). Not for nothing does the New Testament document that speaks most radically about the love of God end in this way. We are ever in danger of making our God the instrument of our violence. If, finally, we turn to Father in time of need, at the moment when the little enclosed worlds we have made are falling apart, we find looking back at us, not the face of Crucified who loved us and gave himself for us, but a monstrous projection of our own unredeemed desire. We find, too late, that we have been making God in our own image. Our sorry religion has become a mirror reflecting back to us, not our faith, but our attempts to evade it.

All this is very human, but so is God. The Father has patience with our whole wandering course. But in the abundant economy of his supreme gift, there are many gifts; what I suggest is that Mary is given to us in the communion of the saints to lead us back to the centre, to keep our faith ever on track, moving into the trackless expanses of the infinity of love and mercy. Heaven has been opened so that even now we might live there, no longer suffocated by the poisoned air of our inhuman history. Heaven has been opened that we might breathe anew, not the stale atmosphere of our old violent idols, but the free air of God's peaceable kingdom; there to find that words like peacemaking, forgiveness, compassion and praise of God are not the ethereal waftings of those who turn their backs on the world, but the real language of the Word of God made flesh amongst us.

Let me offer an example from the classics of Christian literature, Dante's *Commedia Divina*.[4] Though he is lost in the woods (*Inf.* I), the poet can glimpse the light on the hilltop, but a keen sense of his immersion in the sinfulness and violence of the world is preventing him from approaching it: 'Midway through the journey of our life I found myself in a dark wood, where the right way was lost.' Another poet, the pagan Vergil, representing what is best in the squalid violent history of Rome, Italy and its culture, comes to his rescue (poets, it seems, stick together!) He explains that he has sent by the beloved Beatrice—who was sent by Lucia, who in turn was sent by Mary who had compassion on him in his confused state. Beatrice explains to Vergil, 'A gracious lady sits in heaven grieving/ for what has happened

---

4. Here I am indebted to the researches of Professor David Gill, SJ, of Boston College.

to the one I send you to,/ and her compassion breaks heaven's stern decree' (II, 85). Compassion from above begins a conversion from below. Vergil leads Dante through Hell where he learns to acknowledge his sinfulness; thence to Purgatory to be purified of all that obscures his sight. But culture, art and history, represented in Vergil, can go no further. The gifts of grace and heavenly wisdom take over in the person of Beatrice who leads him on the way to Heaven. As he ascends through increasing levels of illumination and love for God, he is hampered by the theological conflicts that tie him to the world he is leaving. How is God both merciful and just? How is human freedom compatible with divine predestination? How is the perfection of God related to this imperfect universe? How is God outside all time and space and yet wholly present to every place and time? Though still perplexed by such problems, he keeps moving on to the fuller evidence that can come only in a higher wisdom and a greater love.

There comes a point where Beatrice leaves him (*Par* XXXI), to hand him over to St Bernard, the great contemplative and devotee of Mary. Bernard points him to Mary in her highest position in the mystical rose and explains to him the various ranks of the saved (XXXII). When Bernard prays to Mary for him (XXXIII, 1–39), Mary smiles on Bernard and without a word turns her gaze 'into the Eternal Light' (43). There follows a burst of illumination for Dante himself:

> Bernard then gestured to me with a smile/ that I look up, but I already was/ instinctively what he would have me to be . . . /
> And from then on my vision rose to heights/ higher than words, which fail before such a sight/ and memory fails too at such extremes. (49–57).

Following the direction of Mary's gaze, into the eternal light, words fail him before the boundless mystery of God's love:

> Then a great flash of understanding struck/ my mind, and suddenly its wish was granted./ At this point failed high fantasy/ but like a wheel in perfect balance turning,/ I felt my will and my desire impelled/ by the Love that moves the sun and the other stars (140–145): *L'amor che muove il sole et le altre stelle.*

It would seem that Mary mediates the only way beyond the violent, limited antagonistic patterns of understanding reality, to gaze into the mystery into which she has been enfolded. In this sense she 'is breaking heaven's stern decree', drawing us from the fatal dynamics of idolatrously sanctioned violence into luminous world of the divine mystery itself. In the poet's journey she is present at the beginning and the end. And yet in the whole inspired account of his journey, from his mid-life crisis in the dark wood to his surrender to love that has been revealed, Mary does not speak a word. Still, for Dante and for the millions of his fellow believers Mary does 'mean the world' in a unique way. The Blessed Virgin Mother of God incarnates dimensions of meaning that cannot be simply put into words, meanings that arise from the deepest feelings of the human heart as faith, hope and love stir within it.

Through communion with Mary we are less likely to fall back into fear, and into the violent projections that make religion an ideology justifying the defensive, divisive force in human culture. And again, in another classic statement, this time from the writings of John 'See what love the Father has given us, that we should be called the children of God; and that is what we are . . . Beloved, we are God's children now; what we will be has not yet been revealed' (1 Jn 3:1–2). As we relate to Mary given to us as our Mother by the crucified Jesus, we come to a deeper sense our ultimate identity as God's children; and by contemplating her Assumption as the gift of the Risen one, we have a sure indication of what we shall be.

This is exactly what Gerard Manley Hopkins was getting at, though unencumbered by the technical language of theology, when he exercised the poet's right to go to the heart of the matter in the great Marian poem, 'The Blessed Virgin compared to the Air we Breathe'.[5] On that May Day holiday at the Jesuit school at Stonyhurst in 1883, Hopkins put up his poem on the notice board, among what he describes as other 'polyglot poems in honour of the BVM'. No doubt this poem, rated by one eminent authority as 'the most penetrating and beautiful Marian poem in our language',[6] was lucky to survive.

---

5. Here I am indebted to Dr Leo M Mangliviti, SJ, '"World-Mothering Air": The Virgin Mary as Poetic Image' in an article recently submitted to *The Hopkins Quarterly*.

6. Norman Weyand, *Immortal Diamond. Studies in GMH* (New York: Sheed and Ward, 1949), 246.

As the title of the poem expresses it, Mary is compared to the air we breathe, 'wild air, world-mothering air,/ Nestling me everywhere/ . . . This needful, ever spent/ and nursing element;/ My more than meat and drink/ my meal at every wink.'

Influenced by Saints Bernard and Louis Grignon de Montfort, he finds in the life-giving atmosphere of this planet an analogy of Mary's gracious presence: 'Now but to breathe its praise/ Minds me in many ways/ of her who not only God's infinity/ dwindled to infancy/ Welcome in womb and breast/ Birth, milk and all the rest/ But mothers each new grace/ That does now reach our race–'

Reflecting on her presence, he writes, 'I say that we are wound/ With mercy round and round/ As if with air: the same/ Is Mary, more by name./ She, wild web, wondrous robe/ Mantles the guilty globe.'

In all this she serves the mystery of Christ rescuing us from the violence of our history, to continue in us his incarnation: 'And plays in grace her part/ About man's beating heart,/ Laying, like air's fine flood,/ The death-dance in his blood;/ Yet no part but will/ Be Christ our Saviour still./ Of her he took flesh:/ He does take fresh and fresh,/ Though much the mystery how/ Not flesh but spirit now/ And makes, O marvellous/ New Nazareths in us,'.

By breathing this Marian atmosphere, in which the mystery of the incarnation is continued, a new human identity is formed as, 'Men may draw like breath/ More Christ and baffle death;/ Who born so, comes to be/ New self and nobler me/ in each one and each one/ More makes, when all is done/ Both God's and Mary's Son.' In that cosmic, womb-like air, the whole Christ is brought to birth. The englobing presence of Mary is the matrix in which meaning of our faith is realised.

In the second section of the poem, Mary figures in Hopkin's poem in something the same way as she influenced Dante in 'breaking heaven's stern decree'. She is an aspect of God's tender incarnation among us. For the poet, when the sky is most blue, the wor0ld is most full of light "When every colour glows/ Each shape and shadow shows." Her role is make the divine 'Much dearer to mankind;/ Whose glory bare would blind/ Or less would win man's mind./ Through her we may see him/ Made sweeter, not made dim,/ And her hand leaves his light/ Sifted to suit our sight.' The poem concludes in a more directly prayerful mode: 'Be thou then, O thou dear/ Mother, my atmosphere/ . . . Stir in my ears and speak there/ Of God's love, O live air/ Of patience, penance prayer/ World-mothering air, air wild/ Wound with thee, in thee isled/ Fold him, fold fast thy child.'

Mary is best known in the poetry and feeling of faith. She is at once a pervasive presence and a many-sided symbol. I suggest we can appreciate this point only if we set our feeling for Mary as the icon of trinitarian love in contrast with a world of other feelings and other images: soured, bitter, violent, vindictive feelings; and images of a world nourishing itself on its own illusions, serving its own idolatrous projections, exhausted in its own fragile self-glorification.

But Mary breathes a purer air and lives in another atmosphere. To express such an awareness, 'devotion' is now too weak a word—as though it were suggesting something peripheral to the Church's life; a mere consolation for the non-intellectual, something vulgar and deviant. But 'the heart has its reasons . . .' In the feeling of faith, and in its poetry, I think we will find her; more to the point, will find her with those who most suffer and feel overwhelmed by life and even religion itself. Theologians might defer to the poets, to the simple faithful who have not learned how to doubt, to those whose hopes stretch beyond words, to the peacemakers and the bringers of mercy, to those who love outstrips all ideologies ; and to this woman who stands with us, and directs our gaze into that realm where 'the fire and the rose are one'—to 'the love that moves the sun and the other stars' (Dante).

The *Salve Regina* ends with three untranslateable words: *O clemens, O pia, O dulcis Virgo Maria.*

On the subject of art, a remark of George Steiner is instructive. He is speaking of the need to enter completely into the world of a work of art as a condition for understanding it. He goes on to say,

> In a wholly fundamental, pragmatic sense, the poem, the statue, the sonata are not so much read, viewed or heard as they are *lived*. The encounter with the aesthetic is, together with certain modes of religious and metaphysical experience, the most 'ingressive', transformative summons available to human experiencing. . . the shorthand image is that of the an Annunciation, of 'a terrible beauty' or gravity breaking into the small house of our cautionary being. If we have heard rightly the wing-beat and the provocation of that visit, the house is no longer habitable in quite the same way as before. A mastering intrusion has shifted the light . . .[7]

---

7. George Steiner, *Real Presences* (Chicago: Chicago University Press, 1996), 143.

The Assumption of Mary

The Catholic doctrine of the Assumption of Our Lady was solemnly defined in 1950. This is one more point where, theologically speaking, the intentionality of faith has hurried past its powers of expression. If Mary is declared to be assumed, body and soul, into heaven, then the corporate, historical authority of the Catholic Church is thereby committed to a view of materiality, corporeality, and physicality in a way that is largely beyond our powers of expression, in either conceptual or even imaginative terms.

Still, in confessing Jesus ascended into heaven Jesus and the assumption of Mary faith stretches forward and upward. Ambrose of Milan expressed the cosmic sweep of the mystery of Christ with the words, 'In Christ's resurrection, the world arose. In Christ's resurrection, the heavens arose; in Christ's resurrection the earth itself arose.'[1] In terms of theological significance, the ascension is the completion and expansion of the incarnation. That enables us to glimpse the connections between the incarnation, the ascension and the universal transformation anticipated in the Catholic doctrine of Mary 'assumed body and soul into heaven'. In that context, the assumption of Mary is a concrete symbol of the overbrimming significance of the ascension of Jesus. Now assumed into the glory of Christ, she is the anticipation of the heaven of a transfigured creation.

In this perspective, Mary is the paradigmatic instance of creation open to, collaborating with, and transformed by, the creative mystery of God in Christ. As the Mother of Christ, she symbolises the generativity of creation under the power of the Spirit. In her, as the Advent antiphon has it, 'the earth has been opened to bud forth

---

1. *De excessu fratris sui*, bk 1. *PL* 16, 1354.

the Saviour'. In its confession of the assumption, Christian hope finds a particular confirmation. In Mary, now assumed body and soul into the heaven of God and Christ, our humanity, our world and even our history have reached their divinely-destined term. She embodies the reality of our world as having received into itself the mystery that is to transform the universe in its entirety. The seer of the Apocalypse invites his readers to share the vision of 'the holy city, the new Jerusalem, coming down out of heaven from God, prepared as a bride adorned for her husband' (Rev 21:1–3). Such a vision is the background for both a theology of the ascension of the one who uniquely descended from on high, and for Mary's assumption as the New Eve and her place in the new creation.

In Mary's assumption, our world is diaphanous to the glory of God, and the great cosmic marriage begins. The Spirit has brought forth in her the particular beauty of creation as God sees it. In her, human history has come to its maturity, its age of consent, to surrender to the transcendent love for which it was destined. Out of such a union, the whole Christ of a transfigured creation is born. Thus, while the focus of Christian hope is in Christ's death, resurrection and ascension, there is a *reprise*, as it were, of the paschal mystery in its efficacy. In the assumption of Mary, the gift of Christ's transforming grace has already been received, and attained its transforming effect. The ascended Christ has conformed her to himself, so that she embodies receptivity to the gift of God—who 'has raised us up with him and seated us with him in the heavenly places in Christ Jesus, so that in the ages to come he might show the immeasurable riches of his grace in kindness towards us in Christ Jesus' (Eph 2:6–7).

Assumed into the heaven of her Son, Mary is no longer subject to the rule of death (1 Cor 15:42–58). Her transformed existence is no more enclosed in the physicality of a world undisturbed by the resurrection and the ascension of the crucified One. United to Christ, Mary lives and acts, and continues to act, as the Mother of the Church. In the heaven of Christ, her intercessory prayer and compassionate involvement has a measureless influence. Invoked as Mother of the Church, Our Lady Help of Christians, Mother of Mercy or Mother of Perpetual Help, Our Lady of Guadalupe (indeed, in all the invocations of the Litany of Loreto, and more), she is present in the divine realm of boundless life and love.

Mary of Nazareth is the name of an historical person—the Mother of Jesus. Yet history has no record of her life except through the documents of faith, above all the Gospels of the New Testament. It is significant in the present context that she has become known to faith only through the immense transformation that took place in the resurrection of her crucified Son, and its impact on human consciousness through faith, hope and love.

Her assumption enables faith to glimpse the 'opened heaven' of Jesus' promise to the disciples in his conversation with Nathanael: 'Amen, amen, I say to you, you will see heaven opened and the angels of God ascending and descending on the Son of Man' (Jn 1:51). Jesus embodies the open heaven of communication between God and creation. In Mary's assumption, the effects of that communication are anticipated in way appropriate to her vocation as Mother of whole Christ, head and members.

In short, the salvific effect of the resurrection and ascension of Christ comes home to the life of faith through the assumption of Mary. Not to recognise this would leave the theology of the ascension of Christ without its most personal effect. Furthermore, if the assumption of Mary is left disconnected from the ascension of Christ, it can quickly become a devotional 'optional extra', and cease to be feature of the universal and cosmic transformation of all creation in Christ.

On the other hand, in the light of the ascension in which the presence and activity of Christ is viewed, belief in the assumption of the Mother of Christ, body and soul, into heaven cannot but continue to inspire a fresh hearing of this exhortation from the Letter to the Ephesians,

> So if you have been raised with Christ, seek the things that are above, where Christ is seated at the right hand of God. Set your minds on the things that are above, not on things that are on earth, for you have died, and your life is hidden with Christ in God. When Christ who is your life is revealed, then you will be revealed with him in glory (Eph 3:1–4).

MESSIAH

The century dies with too many deaths . . .

I survived, I think, a refugee

From successive grey Utopias,

now hesitantly naturalised

in this present place.

Still, you learn something

from the crash-course of history;

—mostly irony after being

Often wrong,

ill-prepared and late.

But what now makes me hesitate

beyond clear borders of love and hate,

is our friend from Nazareth.

A Forum for Theology in the World Vol 9 No 2/2022

May Marian Procession

One clear aspect of the wisdom of Catholic faith is a sense of Our Lady's presence and motherly care. If you could imagine that Mary could be somehow extracted from our Catholic way of life, that life would lose much its colour, warmth and humanity. It would like trying to remove Rosary Hill from our western skyline. Practically every religious order owes a special allegiance to Mary—and a great number name Mary in their official titles. Mary has been the inspiration behind so many saints and holy founders, just as countless shrines and churches have been erected in her honour—and so many places of pilgrimages . . . and processions! It is a feature of Catholic wisdom to stay close to Mary, and with her, to feel the deepest realities of faith more clearly and strongly. With her, we are more completely given over to Christ our Lord—if only for the reason that from the cross he gave her to us to be our Mother. With her we adore the infinite love of God our Father, and rejoice in 'the Lord and giver of life', who is the Holy Spirit. Everything that she has, she has received from God; and everything that she has received makes her belong to us as our Mother.

Our procession this afternoon has a special focus on the icon of our Lady, 'the Seat of Wisdom', *Sedes Sapientiae*. It was especially commissioned a decade ago by Pope John Paul II as a gift to the university students of the world. I am sure that Our Lady would be delighted as we invoke her then as the Seat of Wisdom, and Our Lady of Perpetual Help, and, as the month goes on, as the patroness of Australia, Our Lady Help of Christians. A Catholic imagination has plenty of space for images of Mary, old and new, simply because *she* is not an image, but a living presence inviting us into the depths of God's infinite mystery.

Some years ago, a great project was begun to preserve and restore the wonderful frescoes of Michelangelo that adorn the ceiling of the Sistine Chapel. The years and the centuries had inevitably taken their toll. The paint was cracking, dampness had seeped in, dust and grime had affected the colours. As the project of restoration got under way, every section of that famous ceiling was patiently treated, cleansed and restored to its original brightness. The result was stunning. The colours now glowed, and we, these five centuries later, were able to glimpse something close to that original brilliance of what appeared when Michelangelo put away his brushes, dismantled the scaffold and unveiled his masterpiece.

Like those skilled restorationists of the Sistine ceiling, Mary in her special way hightens our ability to appreciate the original beauty of God's great work of art in Christ. She does not add to the original beauty of God's revelation, but she helps us to see it more clearly. Through the influence of Mary, faith can be cleansed of the grime of routine, the dampness of devotion grown cold and the dust of over-familiarity. At the touch of the Mother of Christ, we see more clearly the wonder of the incarnation, share more deeply in the sacrifice of the cross, and live more gloriously the joy of the resurrection. Standing with her, we adore more surely the life-giving power of the Holy Spirit, leading us to Christ and forming and energising the Body of Christ in the Church. Again, as we pray to Our Lady and our Mother, we sense more intimately the character of God as Our Father. For the fatherhood of God is revealed not only in his beloved Son, but also in this woman chosen to be the Mother of Jesus. Where the Father will say to the disciples on the mountain of the Transfiguration, "This is my Son, the beloved! Listen to him", Mary will tell the attendants at the marriage feast of Cana, 'Do whatever he tells you'.

As already mentioned, today we are honoring the icon of Mary, the Seat of Wisdom, *Sedes Sapientiae*. In its original religious sense, an 'icon' was never regarded simply a devotional picture. It had to produced (or 'written' as they say) in an atmosphere of contemplation and liturgical prayer, entirely intent on allowing the light and beauty of God shine into our world. Icon artists must seek to purify themselves of all self-centredness, so that they will be completely at the service of God's self-revelation. The icon we venerate today, as all others, is a work of prayer as much as of human skill.

Now, while there are innumerable icons of Mary, we can say that she is *in person* an icon of the divine. When we pray to Mary, our faith does not stop with a consoling depiction of this young Jewish woman of long ago. She is not someone made in our image, but the woman made in God's image. Through her the Light came into the world and continues to shine. It is true that some have misinterpreted our Catholic devotion to Mary. They consider that she is not an icon, but an idol, merely reflecting back to her devotees their own feelings, wants and desires. But, we must insist, when true faith sees her as an icon of God's truth and love, she is back-lit by a light not of this world; it shines into our world, not to ratify our all-too-human needs and wishes, but to make our hearts expand to the boundless dimensions of God's loving will.

Mary is no idol; she is a living icon. With her we pray to the Father, not 'may my kingdom come', not, 'may my will be done', but 'may your kingdom come'–and 'let it be done unto me according to your Word'. So, when we contemplate this beautiful icon of 'Mary Seat of Wisdom', we understand first of all that she is in person the living icon of the loving wisdom of God.

But there is a question: what is meant by this word, 'wisdom'? How is it different from the information teeming through our world? How is wisdom different from knowledge in general? The short answer, though a very important one in our world of limitless information, is that wisdom suggests a deep sense of reality as a whole. Wisdom lives at the point where the truth of the mind and the love of the heart meet: the deepest truth is known by love; and love's greatest gift is always the truth. And so, to be wise, is live in the midst of life's questions, ambiguities, light and darkness, with the right sense of proportion—in relation to God, ourselves and our world.

Why is it, then, that we venerate Mary as the Seat of Wisdom? She is the Mother of Christ. In her Son, the gracious wisdom of God has appeared amongst us. Mary leads us to this wisdom incarnate, the Word made flesh. In him all things were made. He is the "light of the world". Jesus from the cross gave us to Mary when, referring to the Beloved Disciple standing there with her, he said, 'Behold your son'. Then, he addressed that special disciple, 'Behold, your mother'. This disciple standing by the cross stands for all the followers of Christ through the ages. Mary is their mother, nurturing and guiding them in the way of true wisdom. The Gospel tells us that this favoured disciple took Mary into his care. Today, we are the beloved disciples of Christ, and in the name of true wisdom, that wisdom that refuses to let the heart grow hard, or the mind shrink to the tiny world of selfishness, we too take Mary into our homes and into our hearts. She lives with us at the deep centre of our lives.

By leading us to her Son, she is bringing us to wisdom—to the wisdom of the mind and to the wisdom of the heart. I have referred to the words of Jesus from the cross. But what does Mary say? The Gospel says nothing of her speaking as she stood by the cross. Earlier in the Gospel, however, at the marriage feast of Cana, she had spoken—in words of perfect wisdom that need no comment: 'Do whatever he tells you'. In such words, she, the first of believers, is communicating her own deepest wisdom.

Of course, we can look in the other Gospels in order to saviour more deeply the wisdom that Mary embodies. Saint Luke, for instance, gives a lively compendium of her wisdom in what comes down to us as the *Magnificat*. It gives some indication of how the first communities of faith treasured the wisdom of Mary.

Hear then the wisdom of Mary: 'My soul glorifies the Lord, my spirit rejoices in God, my saviour'. There is the most fundamental wisdom, to live not locked in ourselves, in our own tiny worlds, but to live out of ourselves for the glory of God. 'My spirit rejoices in God my Saviour.' There too is wisdom, to find one's joy in the joy and bounty of God, to delight in the truth that God is God, and that this God is turned lovingly toward us.

But then there is the wisdom of true humility: 'He looks on his servant in her nothingness, henceforth all ages will call me blessed.' Before God, we are indeed nothing of ourselves; our world is made out of nothing . . . for everything and everyone has been loved into being out of the sheer goodness of God. With the joy of being so loved by God, we can say with her that all the generations that make up the history of world will call her blessed, and us too, blessed as we have been with the infinite treasure of Christ.

'The Almighty works marvels for me; Holy is his name!' The wisdom of Mary leads to the praise of God: all she is, her place in the plan of God is a gift, a sheer gift. It arises from the generosity of the all-Holy God in choosing a woman of our world, a part of creation, to bring forth in time and space and in the air of this planet, a son who is 'God from God, Light from Light, true God from true God'. Holy indeed is the name of this God of wonders, but not as one infinitely remote; for he is compassionately close to us in the mercy that spans all ages—and includes, we must believe, our own: 'His mercy is from age to age on those who fear him.' Mary did not live in a perfect age or among perfect people in a perfect country; but she lived to glorify God in the way God asked and willed.

She shows too the wisdom of acknowledging that God alone is God: 'He puts forth his arm in strength and scatters the proud-hearted.' Before him all human pretence is exposed. The proud-hearted—those so full of themselves that there is no room for God—will be scattered—until they find the wisdom of a humble contrite heart.

God will be God. The Father will glorify his Son; the Son will glorify the Father; and both will glorify their Good Spirit, just as the Holy Spirit will make our hearts restless until we acknowledge the wonder and glory of God. For their good, all the ambitions of the mighty, the rulers of the world, will be brought to nothing; but, in the company of the humble woman of Nazareth, those who entrust themselves to the mighty and merciful hand of God will be lifted up from wherever they have been put down: 'He casts the mighty from their thrones and raises the lowly.'

But wisdom means solidarity with those who most suffer: 'He fills the starving with good things, sends the rich away empty.' As it lifts us up to God, it sends us out to our neighbor in need. We cannot share Mary's wisdom without sharing her compassionate awareness of the needy. The selfish heart, grown cold, empty and dead, feels God's judgment. Those who through greed have forgotten the wider world of suffering, will be left hungering for the only food that matters.

The wisdom of Mary rejoices in the divine providence that guides the people of God in every age—beginning from Abraham, 'our father in faith', through the centuries of Israel's longing from deliverance, to this present time of the Church—and to *our time too*; it is, after all, the only time we have: 'He protects Israel, his servant, remembering his mercy, the mercy promised to our fathers, for Abraham and his descendants forever.' Mary will tell us that God never forgets either his mercy or our need; that mercy is always at work, no matter how dismal the time or how dark the night. God's giving is unstinted. His love has no end. There is nothing in all creation that can separate us from the love he has shown us in Christ Jesus, Our Lord.

St Paul exclaims, 'O the depth of the riches of wisdom and knowledge of God!' (Rom 11:33). His words resonate with the Wisdom teaching of the Old Testament:

> All wisdom is from the Lord, and with him it remains forever. The sand of the sea and the drops of rain and the days of eternity—who can count them? The height of heaven, the breadth of the earth, the abyss, and wisdom—who can search them out? Wisdom was created before all other things . . . the root of wisdom—to whom has it been revealed? (Sir 1:1–5)

The wisdom of God has been revealed to us in Christ Jesus. And it is he, our Redeemer, who has given us Mary to be our mother. May the wisdom of Mary pervade the Church to make strong and wise in proclaiming the Gospel. In this time of darkness and new beginnings, may her wisdom give us the nerve to face, merrily and with boundless hope, the struggles ahead.

Mary, Help of Christians, touch Australia with the grace your wisdom. May we never become a heartless or faithless people, but a land of humanity and hope and hospitality in the midst of the world's sufferings.

Mary, Seat of Wisdom, pray for us.
Sedes Sapientiae, ora pro nobis. Amen

A Forum for Theology in the World Vol 9 No 2/2022

Mary: From Image to Reality

Mary for this third millennium is a challenging topic, and demands in many situations a reclaiming of our Marian Inheritance. Without such a reclamation project, we would risk a kind of amnesia at the very roots of Catholic identity. The presence of Mary is so interwoven with the gift of Christ himself, with the grace of belonging to Church in the distinctive world of its imagination and in the restless direction of its mission. Granting, then, that reclaiming our common Marian inheritance is desirable, how might it be possible? I will be stressing the essential interconnection of our Marian experience with the mystery of God's trinitarian love as it is expressed in the creed. Further, I will be suggesting that the influence of Mary in the consciousness of faith is both liberating and attractive. It works to replace that heart of stone—which projects patterns of violence onto God—with the heart of flesh beating to the rhythms of an always greater grace.

Still, something has to be done, even if there is no place for nostalgia. Every time has its grace: 'a time to break down, and a time to build up; a time to tear and a time to sew; a time to keep silence and a time to speak' (Eccles 3:3, 7). In this new millennium, after a time of breaking down old forms, of tearing old fabrics, of being silent about what we thought was so obvious, it is a time to build, to sew and to speak, that the generations coming after us will have, whatever the world's weather, the sturdy house of faith, the best garments to wear, and the true words to speak. But that will mean diagnosing the problem. The great Marian tradition needs to be set in a larger ecology of informed faith if it is to bear fruit in the years ahead.

Devotion to Mary has been pervasive in Catholic faith and life. Without her, the holy places of pilgrimage would be deserted. The great poem of Christian culture would lack an inspiring image. Parts of the human heart would die. Without this woman our humanity would be diminished. Extract from the Scriptures themselves all Marian reference and association, and they would read far differently. The infancy narratives of Matthew and Luke, the Johannine account of Cana and the Cross, Mary's presence in the company of the disciples on the first Pentecost as described in Acts, resonate with biblical expressions and figures such as Eve, 'the mother of all the living', the ark of the covenant in which God dwelt, the Virgin Daughter of Sion awaiting the fulfilment of divine promises, the Wisdom through which all God's works are accomplished, and even 'the woman clothed with the sun' as described in the Book of Revelation. Take out all these precise references and consider how would the scriptures be read. On the other hand, how should the art of faith melt down the metal of past devotion, purify and recast it, not to fashion it into an idol of pietistic projection, nor even into a beautiful image, but into a more splendid icon of the living God, luminous with the radiance of an infinite love that has given what is most precious to itself for the life of the world?

Let us look more closely at five kinds of problems that have arisen, each one of which calls forth a creative and hopeful solution. First, the Church itself has insisted on reclaiming Mary in a new sense.[1] Vatican II refused to let Marian devotion flourish independently outside the ecology of Church-life. Mary was to be appreciated, not apart from, but within, the whole mystery of the Church, as with the ancient triad *Maria, ecclesia, anima*—Mary, the Church, and the individual believer. Devotion to her, imitation of her, everything divinely realised in her and deriving from her, belongs within the living ecology of the Church itself. She is not an object of optional religious devotion, but one to be celebrated at the heart of ecclesial life, to inspire the People of God, to a new intensity of faith, communion and mission.

Still, a relocation must expect some dislocation. An institutionally-defined Church simply absorb a symbolically-defined Mary. She is not a compensatory figure, someone to hide behind in all our varieties of ossification and spiritual timidity. If the Church is to see herself in Mary, there are consequences in terms of ongoing conversion and surrender to God. This is what Pope Paul VI was getting at, perhaps, when he took the council fathers beyond what they were prepared to

---

1. *Lumen Gentium*, chapter 8.

say, in declaring Mary to be 'the Mother of the Church'.[2] She is our sister in faith within the Church; but she is also our Mother, embodying the meaning of the Church in a way that is not yet fully realised. Mary represents the maternal excess of the grace, love and compassion that always demand a more worthy institutional expression. In this regard, she is not a compensation for our often sorry performance, but a disturbance, even an uncomfortable presence, in the life of the Church, always inspiring something more for us pilgrim people . . .

The second fertile problem, quite intimately associated with the first, is ecumenical dialogue.[3] Let me give one instance. An ecumenical group of pastors and scholars has been meeting at the Trappe des Dombes in Southern France since 1937. Their fundamental conviction has been that reconciliation in the churches will come only through a process of conversion. Despite what they sensed as general taboo on discussing the Marian tradition—Lutheran-Catholic exchanges in the US have been a notable exception—this group has just published the results of the investigations they initiated in 1991. With good Gallic logic, they have divided the subject along the lines of consensus, first, and then areas of divergence.

Interestingly, they decided that the scriptures were not the best place to start. Though eyes might see the same printed marks on the biblical page, hearts and minds see in a different fashion. Different visions are shaped by the preconceptions and sensitivities that history has bred into them. Hence, history emerged as the best starting point. Through investigation of Christian history, not only are their landmines to be cleared, but new places can be discovered, or old places rediscovered in a new way. For example the Immaculate Conception was first defined by the Council of Basle on 15 September 1439, and a feast instituted for the whole church. This was, of course, a good hundred years before what we know as the Reformation, and over 400 years before the eventual definition. Because the papal delegation left the gathering before its conclusion, this Council's decrees were never officially received. Still, it is valuable witness to a consensus in the Western church before the dismemberment which followed. Even at

---

2. Concluding the third session of the Council, 21 November 1963.
3. *Marie dans le dessein de Dieu et la communion des saints.* I. *Dans l'histoire et dans l'Ecriture* (Bayard Editions/ Centurion, 1997); II. *Controverse et conversion*, 1998. See Bernard Sesboüé, SJ, 'Le Groupe des Dombes: Marie dans le dessein de Dieu', in *Etudes*, 3884, Avril 1998: 513–519.

the onset of the Reformation a century later, Marian doctrines were not the crucial issue. Mary and the solemn definitions of the Church were respected by the reformers. Note Luther's lovely hymn: 'She is my love, the noble Maid/ Forget her can I never;/ Whatever honour men have paid/ My heart she has forever.'[4] For the reformers, the excesses of medieval piety were the target in that they distracted from the centrality of Christ and the all-sufficiency of grace. The Protestant position did not radicalise until the eighteenth century, when extreme positions polarised both sides. Excesses of language and devotion accorded Our Lady a quasi-divine status and a virtual omnipotence; and then, while God was left to administer justice, Mary offered the ministrations of mercy. On the other side, following, for instance, the British savant, David Hume (*The Natural History of Religion* (1750), a contrast set in between an elite higher religion of monotheism and the vulgar polytheism of the masses:[5] The vulgar, that is, indeed, all of us, the few excepted, being ignorant and uninstructed, never elevate their contemplation to the heavens so far as to discern a supreme mind or an original providence.

No prizes for guessing where Marian devotion was placed! But at both extremes, Marian devotion was uprooted from the larger ecology of the Church's trinitarian life.

Ecumenical dialogue recognises the creed as the norm for the interpretation of our doctrinal history, to govern a fruitful retrieval of the Marian tradition and the data of scripture itself. The first article of the Creed establishes Mary as a creature with everyone else, a woman of Israel totally dedicated to the praise and worship of God. The second article, dealing with the redemptive incarnation of the Son, is the context in which the Infancy Narratives can and should be interpreted. The third article, dealing with the gift of the Spirit, the communion of saints and the life of the world to come, places her in the life of Trinitarian grace circulating in all believers, living and dead. Within the framework of the creed, the significance of Mary can be explored and celebrated. So much, and it is a great deal, is held in common.

---

4. Quoted in Hugo Rahner, *Our Lady and the Church* (London: Darton, Longman and Todd, 1961), 114.
5. See Peter Brown, *The Cult of the Saints. Its Rise and Function in Latin Christianity* (Chicago: University of Chicago Press, 1981), 13–20.

But there are points of hesitation and divergence. The first deals with the mode of Mary's cooperation in God's redemptive plan. A classically Protestant theology is rightly suspicious of anything that Catholic tradition assigns to her that seems to take away from the all-sufficiency of Christ's mediation. Here Catholic teaching must be careful to emphasise that she too is a beneficiary of her Son's redemption, even though in a primary and exemplary form. As St Augustine pithily said, and his words have application to this issue, 'When God crowns our merits, he is only crowning his own gifts'. What Mary is and does is the result of the sheer gift of God in Christ.

Then there is the vexed question of Mary's perpetual virginity. Though scripture mentions the brothers and sisters of Jesus, though this has long been interpreted along the lines of then culturally dominant reality of an extended family, must Protestant opinion be bound to this view of the perpetual virginity of Mary? Though some Protestants see its radical meaning as Mary' continuing and unreserved dedication to the Jesus. Still, others ask, need it be so literally interpreted, granting that there is no absolute scriptural proof one way or the other. Hence a hesitation and divergence result.

Obviously, too, the later Marian dogmas of the Immaculate Conception (1854) and the Assumption (1950) are a stumbling block for many. On the other hand, it is recognised that the closer these doctrines are aligned to the absolutely central doctrines of the Incarnation, the Resurrection and the Ascension, some presenting difficulties are not so acute.

Then there is the question of intercession. We Catholics tend to pray to everyone, from the Trinity to our guardian angels, from St Mary McKillop to the Blessed Virgin Mary. In the psychology of protestant spirituality, believers pray only to God and Christ, even though all the redeemed may be invoked in some way. Note, in fact, how Catholics too make distinctions. In the Litany of the Saints, we invoke the saints and angels and Our Lady to pray for us in a way that is rather different from prayers to the Trinity or to our Lord. The received distinctions of *latria*, *hyperdulia* and *dulia* need to be re-appropriated and clarified. Above all our prayers need to be set within the larger context of 'Jesus living now to make intercession for us' (Heb 9:24), and of the Holy Spirit 'interceding for us with sighs too deep for words' (Rom 8:26). The prayers of Mary and the saints do not replace that fundamental intercession, but are its outcome and realisation. Again the issue is the utter primacy of God's gift in Christ and the Spirit. The conviction that we are all bound together in a web of intercession is the outcome of God's original grace, not a restriction on it. Mary is not simply remembered in her past role as the mother of Jesus. She is invoked as present in her ever-active role. The communion of saints is not a museum-like pantheon of once living figures. It is a realm of life in which the saints continue their unique mission of bringing Christ to the world.

What has been called 'the Hierarchy of Truths' must govern the patient, reverent dialogue taking place. Here, history is a good teacher. Even Thomas Aquinas did not hold the doctrine of the Immaculate Conception as it was finally defined. He can hardly be said to be wanting in authentic faith. All that can be asked from our Protestant partners in dialogue is this: that they do not deny the legitimacy of the development of Marian doctrines in the Catholic Church, nor dismiss them as contrary to the Gospel. That would leave room for another kind of ecumenical development, signs of which abound. What is at stake, then, throughout the ecumenical experience of today, is the broadest possible appreciation of Mary, grounded in scripture, interpreted in accord with the creed, and retrieving the common ground of the great Tradition that has in fact given rise to different, but now converging, traditions. Mary can thus be appreciated as symbol of unity, not as an emblem of antagonism and division.

The third problem did in fact follow from a more ecclesial understanding of Mary's role in the Church, namely in the social responsibility of the Church for the poor in areas of economic and political oppression. Here Mary of the *Magnificat* emerges in a new way. But in those communities of martyrs and prophets that gave rise to Liberation Theology, a new problem emerged. So great and oppressive were the problems being faced that the universe of grace tended to shrink to dimensions of social action measured by success in the heroic projects of justice that were launched. But 'man does not live by bread alone'. The great Gustavo Gutteriez began to write inspiring books on spirituality. In the face of the huge fundamentalist and Pentecostal inroads into the traditionally Catholic populations of Latin America, the liberationist project, with its emphasis on analysis and action, did not sufficiently allow for the needs of the heart and spirit. The story is not over. The Church has been made more serious and competent in its commitment to the poor. But now those very poor are asking for a new integration of Marian spirituality into the heart of their faith. I mention in passing that our Redemptorist church in Baclaran, the locus of intense Marian devotion, with its Novena which draws 100,000 each Wednesday, became in the crucial times of martial law under the Marcos regime a sanctuary, in more senses than one, for those who protested against the economic greed and political manipulations of the government. There seems to be a lot to be learned from serious study of such experiences, as with the case of the Marian Novena at Thompson Road in Singapore, with nearly twenty thousand attending, a considerable percentage of which are not even Christians! Clearly, Mary's presence to the human heart breaks out of the linear analyses of theology, to give something irreplaceable in the experience of faith—be it faith found or rediscovered, faith confirmed or freshly invigorated.

The fourth problem follows on our remark on liberation. Put it another way, 'Can Mary survive feminism?' Feminism and the larger questions dealing with the liberation of women in society is a movement intrinsically associated with the experience of modern forms of democracy. It poses questions that are at once intellectual, moral, religious and spiritual. It challenges our faith to a deeper conversion under each of these heads. An intellectual conversion – in what for men will mean a new kind of listening: how can we human beings explore more truthfully the creativity of women in human history? How can we understand our humanity more inclusively? Secondly, a moral conversion—in what for men will mean a new range of feeling and responsibility: how can we, men and women, love our neighbour in such a way as to respect the dignity and freedom and creativity of women, and resist everything in our hearts, in our culture and our churches that demeans our sisters, our mothers, our friends, spouses or daughters? Then there is the religious dimension of conversion. Granting that God can only be affirmed through analogy, symbol and metaphor, feminist critics rightly point out that it is a distortion of religious consciousness if only masculine images are employed in a one-sided way. The love and liveliness of God can be brought home to our limited understanding only if the full range of human experience is mined for the a necessary play of images— maternal as well as paternal, sponsal and well as familial, feminine as well as masculine. God can be fittingly adored and praised only if the divine glory is expressed through the spectrum of living human experience. Hence feminist theologians have sought to retrieve the full range of biblical metaphors; sometimes in controversial ways, as say, in Elizabeth Johnson's stentorian *She Who is*. Granting that no one in their right theological mind wants to replace a patriarchal idol with a feminist version of the same, this kind of critique is having considerable influence in liturgical texts and in the writing of hymns—and modern English has to face its peculiar poverty as a vehicle of religious communication.

Finally, there is what I would call the spiritual or interior conversion. At this point, women, in their concrete experience, awaken to the uniqueness of their personhood and vocation and creativity: 'to each is given a manifestation of the Spirit for the common good' (1 Cor 12:7). Traditional church discipline excluding women from official ordination in the Church has, of course, been a bone of contention; and no doubt will continue to be, as large sections of the Church suffer eucharistic starvation. But developments are possible. If even Marian doctrines developed, we cannot but expect that the development of the doctrine and the practice of ministry will develop in God's good time. But to totalise the feminist issue on the matter of ordination is a counsel of despair. Mary herself leads us all into a larger comprehension of the issue, if only for the reason that she was not 'ordained' in any ecclesiastical sense; but she *is* the Mother of Christ, and Mother of the Church.

But to return to the general context of feminism as inspiring an intellectual, moral, religious and spiritual conversion—these four dimensions of conversion are inter-related in the momentous feminist turn taking place in human history in this era. If Mary, or any of her thousand faces, is seen to impede any of these dimensions of conversion, then how can she survive feminism? It is no good pretending that Mary is a modern democratic woman. History is not like that; it must acknowledge the political, cultural, religious, biological and economic limitations inherent in the life of a Jewish woman of two thousand years ago, living in a minor province of the Roman empire. But *she* inhabits a universe of grace and faith. If her presence to the community of faith is reduced to her being nothing more than a compensatory cult-figure designed to assuage the displaced religiosity of anxiety-driven, ignorant and idol-prone populace, if she is stripped of all-revelatory significance in terms of God's self-revelation because such a unique event is declared inadmissable, then why do women, why does anyone, need such superstition?

On the other hand, if she pertains to an event that transcends all cultures and all times, namely the unique self-revelation of God in time, then matters are different. She will belong to all ages in a conviviality of life and love. And whatever the position of women, then or now, she will invite them to find themselves, with her and before God, in this actual world. If, in the words of one woman in the Gospel, she was hailed as 'Blessed among women' (Lk 1:42), is there not a sense that feminism itself will not survive as a beneficent force in human history without Mary as all generations continue to call her blessed (Lk 1:48)?

We come now to the fifth and last problem area. We live today with a keener sense of human subjectivity and inwardness. Scholars affected by the anthropological turn in human studies stress the role of consciousness and the symbols and images at work in all the variety of human cultures. The danger is that the objectivity of faith implodes into mere subjectivism. Les Murray has astutely observed that so much of current reflection on our own country is merely an exercise in image-making.[6] The same problem is abundantly in evidence on the subject of Mary. Theology can be more concerned with images of Mary—'the thousand faces of the Virgin Mary' being the title of a recent book (George Tavard)—than with the real person with whom we believers are united in the communion of saints.

That there are all kinds of deviant and compensatory fabrication of images of Mary—as with everything else – cannot be denied. For that reason, the call of Vatican II insists on placing devotion to Mary within the great laboratory of Spirited image-making, namely, the Church itself. The sacramental and mystical imagination of the Church, deriving from the wondrously parabolic imagination of Jesus himself, draws the exuberant piety of the faithful out of the recesses of private fantasy. It leads into the realm of the public, communicative symbolism of the life of the pilgrim People of God, ever under the imperative to be more converted, in faith, hope and love, to what has been revealed.

---

6. Les Murray, 'The Trade in Images', in *A Working Forest. Selected Prose* (Potts Point: Duffy and Snellgrove, 1977), 344–350.

The Word in becoming flesh enters into the human conversation made up of images, symbols, feelings, aspirations. But the revealed Word comes into the world not simply to stay there, but to restore and elevate that world to the universe of grace. Though God's revelation comes from above, while its aim is to give abundantly 'far more than all we can ask or imagine' (Eph 3:20), though the Lord's cross and resurrection explodes the idols of our cultures, revelation speaks no heavenly language. It works with what is there, not to lose itself in human words and symbols, but to disclose the ultimate life-giving truth of God, and all in God. No doubt in these days of 'virtual reality', and extraordinary expertise in forming images be it in advertising or electronic extension of the senses and the imagination, we are so immersed in images that we find it difficulty to distinguish the image from the reality, the mask from the face, the role from the person, the religious symbol from the revealed mystery. Even morality, once understood to be the core activity of personal conscience, becomes an exercise in image-making—'virtue signalling' and 'political correctness' as we call it. Come up with the acceptable image, conform to the pre-established norm, and you are spared any further thought or any further decision.

In stark contrast, faith does not believe in images, even if it is never without them, and ever creative of images more expressive of the mystery it serves. Faith has its history. Though the horizon of belief is coloured by images, faith sees through them, as it were, to anticipate that end-point when images will be no more, and God will be all in all. In its every moment, faith it is radically about God. This is a point of the utmost importance in the present context. Mary is with us in time because she is with God.

God? In his attempt to explore the divine mystery, St Thomas Aquinas named God as 'sheer to-be' (*Ipsum Esse subsistens*). All else exists in a particular, and, hence, limited way; but only God in limitless 'to-be', utter 'is-ness'. In its four dimensional of existence, the physical universe begins those 13.7 billion years ago. Terrestrial life begins those 4.5 billions years ago, and recognisable human history, having bloomed into the added dimension of spiritual consciousness, starts its course two hundred thousand years ago. Our existence is distended, fragmented, categorised, named and grasped in particular segments and contexts.

For God however there is no such limitation. In the ever actual timeless fullness of sheer 'to be', all is present in its wholeness and completion. God does not have to catch up with our future. For it is our future that has to catch up with the 'total and full possession of endless life' which the 'to-be' of God is. For us, being is past or present or future: for God it all *is, now!*

In our understanding, Mary lived in the past. She lived and died, and vanished from this time-bound world of passing things and events and people. To God, and in God, she is present in her wholeness. At the edges of our sense of the presence of the Risen Christ, at the heart of our dim experience of the communion of saints, in the intimate awareness, perhaps, of the presence of our own dear departed, the fringe of another experience is suggested and evoked. It might lead us to read with new eyes, and to hear with new ears, the message of the Gospel. In the imagination of Jesus himself, God was the loving mystery of endless life, the eternal spring of sheer deathless vitality to whom the limits of our lives were not limits at all. To the wily exegesis of the Sadducees, Jesus replied, 'You know neither the scriptures nor the power of God . . . Have you not read what was said to you by God, "I am the God of Abraham, of Isaac, and the God of Jacob"? He is the God, not of the dead, but of the living' (Mt 22:29–33).

God is, therefore, the God of the living Mary. In that timeless, deathless abyss of Life, Mary lives—'assumed into heaven' as we say. The traces of her life in this world recorded in the Gospels, the traces of her presence in the Church celebrated in all the wealth of its Marian experience—all evoke her living presence to us because of her being in God, in the all-encompassing creative mystery of trinitarian love. Our relationship to her is not simply an exercise in devout remembrance, or a matter of endlessly refashioning the huge glittering mass of Marian images and symbols. For she is present to us, and we to her, in the unity and vitality of the Holy Spirit. As that Spirit inspires faith and hope and love in our hearts, it gives a new sense of reality. Illumined by the Light of God, our consciousness embraces her reality, and the reality of all who dwell in the light, as come to fulfilment in the depths of God. We must not get lost in the jumbled ciphers of history, for faith, though it exists in history, lives from beyond history to breathe the air of what is not of this world.

In the words of one of the world's great poets, Paul Celan, 'A Rumbling: truth/ itself has appeared/ among human kind/ in the very thick/ of their flurrying metaphors'.[7]

The Mother of the Lord introduces us to the 'timeless goodness' of her Son. Through her, we understand more clearly how the Word has become flesh in the 'very thick of [our] flurrying metaphors'. In the imagination of faith, the mysteries throw light on one another; human experience is mined for a fund of images to express what lies essentially beyond all adequate expression; and the pilgrimage of faith and hope strains forward to what it already loves, to the promised fulfilment in what no eye has seen, nor ear heard nor the human heart conceived (1 Cor 2:9).

From generation to generation, let the great company of believers enter more and more fully into communion with Mary, and come to appreciate her more deeply as the ever-present icon of trinitarian love, and as the living symbol of the Church itself. Even when we are long departed from this world into the abyss of endless life, there will not be lacking sisters and brothers in the faith who will pray as we pray, even if in the daily life of a world far different from our own, 'Hail Mary, full of grace, the Lord is with thee! Blessed art thou among women'.

---

7. Paul Celan, *Poems*, translated by M Hamburger (Manchester: Carcanet, 1980), 203–204.

Mary, Icon of Trinitarian Love—The God-bearer

In Christian history, Marian doctrines did not emerge till some centuries had passed, for example, the Council of Ephesus (431) when Mary is declared to be *Theotokos*, the God-bearer. The Church was indeed busy with other matters. A huge doctrinal development was in progress, as was evidenced in the early councils of Nicaea, Ephesus and Chalcedon in the first five centuries. The issue was Christian realism. Christian thinkers had indeed allied themselves with the *logos* of the great pagan philosophers in their common concern to leave behind the lurid, polytheistic extravagances of ancient mythologies in order to know the One, the True and the Good. But faith could not rest there. The data of revelation demanded that faith seek its proper understanding by pushing beyond what even the best of philosophy had to offer. The task of theology was to elucidate the reality of the *Agape* that had been revealed, exploding all prior conceptions of God. For the divine *Logos* was incarnate. The life, suffering, death and resurrection of the Lord was now the defining point from which the reality of God had to be affirmed.[1]

In the current philosophical terms, God who had to be solitary in his perfection, and in no way related to the world of flesh and blood and suffering. But this Christian thing was something else. In the light of the Incarnate Word the very notion of God had to change. For the self-giving love of the Son had revealed the originating love of the Father, giving what is so intimately his own, his only Son and his own Spirit, for the world's salvation. What, then, needed to be clarified and affirmed was that God had such a self to give.

---

1. See Anthony J Kelly, 'Mystery and Definition', in *The Trinity of Love. A Theology of the Christian God* (Wilmington, Del: Michael Glazier, 1989), 59–64.

Contrary to the great Greek tradition of philosophy, the Christian meaning of God implied that God was not unrelated to the world in sublime unconcern for the world of its creation as the philosophers had taught. Nor was the divine a self-enclosed monad, existing in the solitude of its own perfection. The faith that through this time had prayed, celebrated, suffered and reflected now demanded that God be conceived in completely un-Greek terms. The divine mystery was one of self-giving love. God was never ultimately alone. Divine perfection was to be found in terms of communion of Father, Son and Holy Spirit. The divine three were inter-related in an inexhaustible vitality into which the world is being drawn. Living in that circle of trinitarian life, the Church already experienced the reality of eternal life.

Christian theology thus began to realise the limitations of philosophical solutions, metaphorical descriptions and uncritical biblicism. It was a movement as much into reverent unknowing of faith as into its definition. The eternal vitality of the three persons of the Trinity circulated in a pattern of unreserved self-giving of each to the other. This was discerned to be the source and form and goal of God's creative and redeeming action in time, so that Jesus can pray, '. . . that they may all be one. As you, Father, are in me, and I in you, may they also be in us, that the world may believe that you have sent me' (Jn 17:21).

In self-communicating dynamism of the divine 'Love-Life', The Father was understood as the infinite original lover, expressing himself in the Word and communicating his love in the Spirit. This sense of the eternal being-in-love was the matrix from which the doctrine of the Trinity emerged into the consciousness of the Church. Theology now had at its disposal a language in which to express in utterly realistic terms the great statements of John: 'Everyone who loves is born of God and knows God. Whoever does not love does not know God, for God is love' (1 Jn 4:7f).[2]

It is little wonder, then, that a full-blown, full-bodied appreciation of Mary as *Theotokos*, as the virginal God-bearer, emerges at this point of marvellous clarification. Only when the great poem of Christian faith had found a consistent doctrinal vocabulary enabling it to break free from pagan myths and traditional philosophy could the context

---

2.   See Kelly, *The Trinity of Love*, 141–173.

be established in which Mary could be venerated. There would be no going back to the goddess-worship that Israel had rejected in the surrounding regions with their fertility goddesses and the practices of ritual prostitution (Cana and Syria has Anath, Astarte and Asherah, the Balylonians had Ishtar, Phrygia had Cybele, the Great Mother, and Egypt had quite a pantheon of female deities (Hathor, Matit, Medfet, Wadjet, and the goddess of learning, Nekhbit, and, above all, Isis).[3] In New Testament times, Paul's preaching provoked a fierce reaction in Ephesus (Acts 19) when he was interpreted as threatening the cult of Artemis (or Diana as she was called in Rome). Demetrius, the silversmith who was part of the roaring trade in little statues of the goddess, denounced Paul and his associates for undermining both the place of the great local temple worship and, of course, for posing a threat to his profits: 'Great is Artemis of the Ephesians' was the indignant slogan. The growing Christian veneration of Mary did not make her a rival to the temple goddesses, not was she a substitute for a female deity. She belonged to a different order of reality. In the Christian scheme of things she had her own place – as a creature, an historical woman, as one redeemed, yet uniquely positioned within the enactment of the Mystery of the Word made flesh amongst us (Jn 1:14). She is the first to know that 'God gives the Spirit without measure' (3:34). As the theology of God developed, so did the theology of Mary along with it.

The classic confession of faith, known to us today as 'the Nicene Creed', can be taken as an unfolding of the meaning of John's statement, 'God is love' (1 Jn 4:8, 16).[4] Now, in that creed there are seven key terms, each irreplaceable if any adequate confession of God as love is to be given: *Father* (the primordial originality of love in being and action), *Son* (the self-gift and self-expression of divine love), *Cross* (the unconditionality of such love), *Resurrection* (the transforming victory of this love), *Spirit* (the ever-expanding gift of God's love), *Church* (the community of love in history), and *heaven*—'the life of the world to come'—(the eschatological consummation of all in love).

Though such terms can be translated in different ways and be differently ordered, though the realities they refer to can never be

---

3. See the informative section in the comprehensive George H Tavard, *The Thousand Faces of the Virgin Mary* (Collegeville MN: Liturgical Press, 1996), 221–247.
4. See Anthony J Kelly, *The Creed by Heart. Relearning the Nicene Creed* (Melbourne: Harper Collins, 1996).

separated in the hologram of the Christian mystery, the creed opts for its own distinctive sequence in articulating the truth of love. Under each of these seven headings, I propose to make a brief comment on Mary to suggest perspectives quite fundamental to our understanding of her presence to us in the faith of the Church.

In the name, *Father*, it is implied that 'God is love', first of all, in an eternal and primordial begetting of the Son through the power of the Spirit, and consequently, as the all-encompassing, sovereignly free source of the being of the universe: 'Not that we loved God . . . 1 Jn 4). An original love precedes all human effort and all created structures and dynamics. Such love is the purely, sheerly, limitless 'given' in relation to all Christian life and action—and indeed for 'all that is . . .'.

The manner in which the Gospels and the creed speak of the Father as the 'first divine person' enables us to ask how Mary is now for us a living icon of the divine, as Mother of God, *theotokos*. How does the motherhood of Mary affect our sense of the Fatherhood of God? In the long history of Catholic and Orthodox liturgical and spiritual traditions, the answer is found only on a lived, implicit level. The current ecumenical re-appraisal of the place of Mary in Scripture and tradition, along with the best influences of the feminist turn in theology, promises a richer understanding.

But, first, Mary receives. Though what we Catholics have come to call her 'immaculate conception', Mary is preserved free from all stain of original sin. This is really a way of formulating her position in the universe of grace:

> Blessed by the God and Father of our Lord Jesus Christ, who has blessed us in Christ with every spiritual blessing in the heavenly places, just as he chose us in Christ before the foundation of the world to be holy and blameless before him in love (Eph 1:3–4).

By being freed from the original sin manifest in the murderous violence and exclusion of others, having nothing within her to close her in herself, Mary is open to the totality of God's plan for creation, to be a pure generative influence in our history. Thus she is destined to be the Mother of whole Christ, head and members, the New Eve, 'the mother of all the living' (Gen 3:20), and to be 'perfect' in mercy as our Heavenly Father is (Matt 5:48; Luke 6:36).

Though conformed to the Father's merciful will, she is in no sense divine. All her grace has been received. But in the universe of grace she is God's most gifted creation. As full of grace and freed from sin, she is the chosen associate of the eternally generative Father to become, in the fullness of time, the human Mother of his Son: 'For the Mighty One has done great things for me . . .' (Lk 1:49).

Her receptivity to the Father results in a unique activity, to be the *Theotokos*, the 'God-bearer'. When we confess that she is 'the Mother of *God*', we mean that she is the human mother of the Word made flesh. She is related to the second divine person as a mother to a son. Because past thinkers have tried to avoid the implication that she was mother of her Son on the divine level of his existence, i.e., in his divine nature, they found themselves saying that she is only the mother of his body or of his human nature. But this ends up being very odd language: no mother is ever a producer of a nature or a body, but the source and term of a unique personal love. The physical, generative aspect of motherhood occurs within the world of persons. In this regard she is related to her son in who he is, in his radical identity as 'God from God, Light from Light'. The fifteen billion year genesis of the universe, in its passage from matter to life, from life to consciousness and freedom, from freedom to Israel's faith in God at work in all things, culminates in her consent. What was in the beginning in the eternal procession of the Son from the Father, now has a new beginning in the history and fabric of the cosmos itself. The eternally begotten Son is really brought forth, born into the world of creation, subjected to it. 'Born of a woman' (Gal 4:4), he would know poverty, live in surrender to God, enter into the risk of living for the Kingdom of God—and suffer the consequences. Having this human mother means that the divine Son is not posturing in a humanity, but is the enhumanisation of the divine in the pain, darkness and joy of human existence. In the womb of Mary, the world holds a divine reality within it: the Mother of Jesus is the Mother of God.

As bringing forth the Christ in the power of the Spirit, Mary can be contemplated as an icon of the Father. Through her Immaculate Conception she is located in that realm of mercy in which God so loves the world. By giving her consent at the Annunciation to be the Mother of the holy one (Lk 1:38), in her initiative in visiting Elizabeth, in the celebration of all-upturning grace in the her *Magnificat*, in bringing forth her child, in pondering the mysteries of God in her heart (Lk 2:19), in sword that pierces her heart in giving what is most intimately her own for the world's salvation, she participates in the generative love of the Father. The Father's declaration at the moment of the Transfiguration, 'This is my beloved Son, listen to him' (Mk 9:7) is echoed in her command, at the marriage feast of Cana: 'Do whatever he tells you' (Jn 2:5). The silent love of her life leads her to the Cross, where she stands with the Beloved Disciple. In that hour of glory, her Son gives his disciple to her, and her Jesus gives to him. Standing with the larger group of disciples at Pentecost, the Spirit which comes from above onto the early Church, is the Spirit that came upon her at the beginning of Jesus' life amongst us.

In all this she embodies the compassionate, life-giving love of the Father. For the generations that have addressed her as Mother, she expresses the tenderness of the Father who has given what is most intimately his own for our sake, as she brings forth the one whom the Father begets. In her way, she gives what the Father has given. She acts in the power of the Spirit with which the Father acts, to give her son for the world's salvation: 'God's love was revealed among us in this way. God sent his only Son into the world that we might live through him. In this is love, not that we loved God, but that he loved us and sent his Son to be the atoning sacrifice for our sins' (1 Jn 4:9–10).

In giving and loving in her human maternal manner, she is the eminent human expression of the Father's love. Against the distortions of religious fantasy, Mary embodies a corrective to any excessive masculinisation of the divine. Is there no significance in the fact that parental role of the Father is expressed in history through the love of a mother. No doubt cultures tend to domesticate the divine in a mono-dimensional fantasy apt to nourish its narrow ideologies. But no particular name, even one as important as that of 'Father' can be so absolutised as to curtail the whole play of language in its celebration of the infinities of God's life and love. In no social or cultural context is reference to God simply a matter of semantics or dead metaphors. If faith is to remain alive to the living God, our language needs to be restlessly imaginative if it is to serve the Word and communicate in the Spirit and express the loving initiative of the Father.

In it use of the word and metaphor of *Son*, 'God is love' in a unique self-utterance and self-expression. In the incarnation, a climactic self-involvement of God in creation takes place. Here God is not so much doing something for us and our salvation, but becomes personally involved with us in the sphere of creation: God-with-us in the Word made flesh and living among us (1:14). God so loves the world as to give what is most intimate to the divine life and most expressive of the divine identity into the flesh of our existence: 'This is my beloved Son: hear him!' (Mk 9:7).

How does Mary embody the self-communicating character of God's love? Here, too, Mary is both passive and active. She receives all from her Son as the first of the redeemed, receiving the totality of the Word made flesh into the faith and flesh of her existence. Yet, in so receiving – for apart from him, along with all believers, she can do nothing (Jn 15:5)—she acts in the most intimate association with her Son's mission, typified in her instruction to the servants at Cana, 'Do whatever he tells you' (Jn 2:5). In her, the words of Jesus are verified: 'My Father is glorified by this, that you bear much fruit and become my disciples' (Jn 15:8). The fruit distinctive of the New Eve as she stands by the cross is expressed in her Son's instruction to her: 'Woman, behold, your son!' (Jn 19:26), when the 'son' here is the Beloved Disciple, the embodiment of immediate and unreserved faith. Jesus gives her to him, not as a sister in the new family of God, but as a Mother: 'Behold, your Mother' (Jn 19:27).

Thirdly, we confess that God is love in the light of the *Cross*. God's love is unconditional and without reserve. It keeps on being love even in the deepest darkness of the world's evil. At the point where the evil of human history is most manifest in crucifying the Son, there love keeps on being love as limitless mercy: 'Father, forgive them for they do not know what they are doing' (Lk 23:34). 'The violent victimisation of worldly power is radically unmasked and subverted.[5]

How does Mary embody the unconditional character of crucified love? Once more, Mary receives and acts. She stands at the foot of the cross as the unique recipient of God's creative merciful love, as acclaimed by Gabriel to be uniquely favoured (Lk 1:28, 30). In following her Son in his mission, she has suffered the piercing of soul that Simeon foretold (Lk 2:35). She has been given the Beloved Disciple by the dying Jesus (Jn 19:26). To her and on this disciple gathered at the foot of the cross as representatives of the new community of faith, the Spirit of Jesus has been given: 'Then he bowed his head

---

5. On this theme, following the thought of René Girard, Gil Bailie, *Violence Unveiled. Humanity at the Crossroads* (New York: Crossroad, 1997).

and handed over the Spirit' (Jn 19:30). A new community of selfless love has been born, the very form of eternal life. It witnesses against the violent idolatrous self-promotion of this world and its 'ruler' (Jn 14:30; 16:11), and refuses to be drawn into the violence of this world. And so Mary receives that she might act, and be a Mother of Mercy in the experience of faith, giving what is most intimately her own for the salvation of the world.

She represents the gentle, vulnerable but ever-persistent presence of that other kingdom. In the words of Jesus: 'My kingdom is not from here . . . For this was I born, and for this I came into the world, to testify to the truth. Everyone who belongs to the truth listens to my voice' (Jn 19:36–37). In Pilate's perplexed response, 'What is truth?' (Jn 19:38), the self-glorifying power of the world relegates this other kingdom, this other realm of life, to what is unreal in the real world of manipulative image-making and ruthless power. In its vocabulary words such as mercy, forgiveness, compassion, humility, adoration, praise, thanksgiving, obedience to God, patience, hope, self-sacrifice, love of others, eternal life, peace, truth and goodness—in short, the language of the beatitudes tend not to figure in the languages of electioneering, media appearances or in politics generally. In a culture of self-promotion this kind of faith, humility and self-giving love is useless.

But Mary has belonged to the truth and heard its voice. Praying to her 'now and at the hour of our death' tends to restrain us from seeking a kingdom of this world with all its panoply of idolatrous pride and violence. In such a world, love is vulnerable, with God only to provide support and justification. But Mary lives as a witness to the truth to which her Son testified. To this degree, to the self-promoting competitiveness and latent violence of a culture powered by the seven deadly sins she is something of a threat. The woman of the Magnificat, praising God for scattering 'the proud in the thoughts of their hearts', and bringing down 'the powerful from their thrones' (Lk 1:51–52) has become a subversive presence.[6]

Fourthly, faith demands that we speak of the *Resurrection*: God is love in a way that shows that such love is divine. Though never reduced to the level of worldly power, it does have its own radiant outcome. It

---

6. See René Coste, *The Magnificat. The Revolution of God* (Quezon City: Claretian Publications, 1987).

is not defeated by the domain of evil and death. It triumphs in raising Jesus from the dead. Lifted up from the earth, the crucified Son draws all to himself (Jn 11:52; 12:32), to be glorified as the true form, source and exemplar of a 'love that bears all things, believes all things, hopes all things, endures all things'—and in the 'love that never ends' as God's greatest gift (1 Cor 13:4–8).

How is Mary related to the power of Resurrecting love? Paul wrote to his Corinthian audience: 'Now if Christ is proclaimed as raised from the dead, how can some of you say there is no resurrection from the dead? If there is no resurrection from the dead, then Christ has not been raised, then our proclamation has been in vain and your faith has been in vain' (1 Cor 15:12–15). With the celebration of Mary's assumption into heaven, faith in the resurrection of the Lord finds a correlative symbol. The power of the resurrection has flowed into the existence of this pre-eminent believer, to transform her being and to perfect her mission. The completeness of her assumption into a mode of bodily life which, following Paul's indirect description of a risen existence (1 Cor 15:42–58), is not subject to the rule of death, nor to the dishonour inevitable in the realm of worldly glory, nor to the weakness that worldly power consigns it. It is not enclosed in physicality of a world undisturbed by the creative imagination of God's Spirit. In her union with her Son as 'the resurrection and the life' (Jn 11:25), she grounds faith in its radical, defiant and universal hope: 'If for this life only we have hoped in Christ, we are of all people most to be pitied. But in fact Christ has been raised from the dead, the first fruits of those who have died' (1 Cor 15:19).

Having received into herself the power of the resurrection, Mary lives and acts. God is not the God of the dead, but of the living (Mt 22:32). How she has acted and continued to act, in a prayer, a presence and a compassion emanating from the heart of the divine abyss: 'Surely, from now on, all the generations that call [her] blessed' (Lk 1:48). Invoked as Our Lady Help of Christians, as the Mother of Mercy and of Grace, as the Mother of Perpetual Help—indeed, in all the invocations of the Litany of Loreto—she is established in realm of endless life with God. She anchors faith, inspires hope, and exemplifies the love inherent in the life that never ends (1 Cor 13:8). In her risen life, assumed into heaven, she is the New Eve, the Mother of all the living: 'Woman, behold, your son' (Jn 19:28). Mary of Nazareth is the name of an historical person—the Mother of Jesus. History has no records of her life except through the documents of faith, above all the Gospels of the New Testament. She has become known to faith only through the immense transformation that affected human consciousness in the resurrection of her Son.

Fifthly, God is love as communicative in the *Spirit*. The love that has originated in the Father, and been incarnate in the life, death and resurrection of the Son, has been breathed into history as a field of new life. It comprehends every time and place and people. In the Spirit, 'the Lord and giver of life', Christ is conceived, the Church brought into being, and all creation moves in a new energy toward its fulfilment. In all creation groaning in its great act of giving birth, in the groaning of Christian faith and love awaiting its full evidence, there is another groaning: 'Likewise, the Spirit helps us in our weakness; for we do not know how to pray as we ought, but that the very Spirit intercedes for us with groanings beyond all utterance' (Rom 8:26).

How Mary related to the gift of the Spirit? By receiving the gift of God, and acting in its power. Through the Spirit, the Father has begotten the Son in eternity. Through the Spirit acting in Virgin Mary, the Father begets his only Son in time. In the words of Gabriel, 'The Holy Spirit will come upon you, and the power of the Most High will overshadow you' (Lk 1:35). In hailing her as the 'the Blessed *Virgin*', faith is expressing two things. First, God's act of self-giving is not restricted or conditioned by what creation can produce in terms of human reproduction or generation. She instances in her mission the initiative of the Spirit in regard to all the children of God, 'who were born, not of blood or the will of the flesh or the will of man, but of God' (Jn 1:13). In confessing her as the *Virgin* Mary, the creed invites us to adore the unique capacity of the divine freedom to bring forth the new, the culminating reality of God-with-us, the Word made flesh, in everyone who 'is born of the Spirit' (Jn 3:8). The genesis of the divine Word in the human world is outside the genetic capacity of any created process. The fullness of Christ is not a product of nature or of human impulse or decision, but the effect of the Spirit. Secondly, when love comes to dwell with us it transforms all it touches, including this Jewish woman, Mariam. She is passive to the Spirit, yet acts in the power of the Spirit, since she has been chosen to be the human created collaborator in the incarnation itself. To her is given a unique 'manifestation of the Spirit for the common good' (1 Cor 12:7). For by the power of the Spirit, Jesus is born of the Virgin Mary. Inspired by the Spirit, her faith defines her being: she is pure receptivity to the Spirit, pure attention to the Word, pure adoration of the Father: 'My soul magnifies the Lord . . .' (Luke 1:40). She is defined in no other way, by no other relationship—neither by a human partner, nor by social expectations. What determines her existence is solely what God can be and what God can do—by who God is for her and who she is for God. She is the woman who most intimately knows that 'for God nothing is impossible' (Lk 1:37). Thus, in her Spirit-formed existence is inscribed the conviction that the gift of God is given out of divine freedom, not as a result of human merit or ambition or evolution or historical development. In her, divine freedom communicates with a created freedom. Divine Love calls for a human love in be its partner in the world's transformation.[7]

Mary's virginal receptivity to the Spirit implies neither a glorification nor a demeaning of human sexuality. In naming Mary as the Virgin Mother of the Lord, the creed is essentially confessing the sheer grace of God, the divine ability to bring about a new creation. Whatever beauty and generativity there may be in human eros, such love does not simply bring God down from heaven, to make the divine either our instrument or our property. God comes because the Spirit gives. And the Spirit so acts because God freely loves and chooses to do so. And in choosing to do so, God inspires a freedom in the other, the Virgin Mary, to receive and cooperate.

The Blessed Virgin is invoked within an horizon that refuses to impose any limits on the Spirit and the divine imagination. Outside of the mystery enveloping her, she cannot be known. Consequently, her virginity has meaning only within the universe of grace. At this point, faith must learn its own reserve. There is no place for any form of theological voyeurism, in a vain effort to reduce God's 'impossible ways' to the humanly familiar. The virginal vocation of Mary becomes apparent only in the light of the resurrection of the Son and the outpouring of the Spirit. It belongs to a new language of the world's transformation in Christ. Love has broken through as the sovereign power at work in the universe.

In that light, faith turns to Mary, the Mother of Jesus, standing with the disciples at Pentecost (Acts 1:14), to recognise her unique

---

7. See Anthony J Kelly, *An Expanding Theology. Faith in a World of Connections* (Sydney: EJ Dwyer, 1993), 171–172.

role in the self-communication of God. In her virginity is embodied the intensity of surrender to the Spirit now demanded of all believers. By acknowledging her virginity, the creed reaches another point of faith's deliberate 'un-knowing' of the mystery. God must be let free to be God – in giving the impossibly gracious gift we most need, even as it remains outside our control, our comprehension and our merits. At such a limit, the virginity of Mary is an icon of the Spirit, not an emblem of body-negating asceticism.

The Spirit active in all creation and in all generations through history brings that creation and that history to a unique point of freedom in this woman. She consents on behalf of all creation to receive into itself the mystery from which all existence derives. She is the world's overture to the power of the Holy Spirit. Within the totality of the world, as a woman named within the history of her people, Mary, the daughter of Sion, a woman of Israel, she is the pre-eminent believer in her Son. All the faithfulness of generations before her and after her, all their waiting on God and their yielding to the Spirit, are condensed in her: 'Be it done unto me according to your Word' (Lk 1:38). She is creation's Yes to both its future and its past. Her *fiat* is the word of youthful enthusiasm and radical acceptance (Lk 1:38)—in contrast to starker expressions of resignation to the divine will in the shadow of the cross. The Holy Spirit, though not reducible to any created power, nonetheless acts within the powers and freedom of creation: the incarnation comes about both from beyond and yet from within the realm of creation. As theology would say, precisely because the divine power so transcends the created order, it can work so immanently within to it. Though the Son is incarnate by the power of the Spirit, he is still truly 'born of the Virgin Mary'.

Sixthly, there is the *Church*: believing that 'God is love' has an historical meaning, from generation to generation, in the life and celebration of the Church as the 'the People of God'. In the community of believers, baptised into the death and resurrection of Christ Jesus, nourished by his body and blood, animated by his Spirit, the love of God is expressed. In the pilgrim, sacramental reality of Church, the saving mystery is celebrated and offered to the world. In its community and mission, the Church is an open circle, living and witnessing to the universal grace of love at work in all lives. To that degree, the Church is that part of world and creation which is alive to the 'impossible' extent of God's love.

How is Mary related to the Church? As a member of the community gathered in the power of the Spirit around the cross of her Son, she was eminently the woman of faith. Her self-surrendering Yes to the design of God, her life of prayer and compassion, carry over to her presence with the disciples awaiting the outpouring of the Spirit that had so possessed her from the beginning. By receiving with the Church she acts in and for the Church. She is remembered in the early communion of faith as the Mother of the crucified and risen Jesus. She stands in that early tradition as the woman living at the end of the history of her people's longing for its Saviour, for the Christ that would be born, and for the Spirit to be poured out on all flesh. In her, 'the Virgin Daughter of Sion', all the hopes and faith of her people are condensed. Elizabeth, summing up the Old Testament praise of the faithful, proclaims, 'Blessed is she who believed that there would be a fulfilment of what was spoken to her by the Lord' (Lk 1:45). While she is an end, a final point, she is also a beginning. Through her consent, in her yielding to the Spirit, the Word adored in her faith is conceived in her womb. Through her, God enters the world. She is the God-bearer, *Theotokos*. Henceforth her whole life and destiny are bound up with her Son, given over to the mystery of who he is and what he means, both then, now, and for future ages.

In this regard, she is a corporate symbol of ecclesial identity. She is not primarily an object of private devotion, nor an occasion for superfluous fantasy. She is given to the representative beloved disciple as his Mother. When he takes her into the intimacy of his heart and home, something happens for the Church. The communion of saints is immeasurable enriched. The hope of Church is securely anchored in the glory of one of our own—this woman who most represents our faith. The Church beholds itself in Mary's grace, thus understanding her assumption as an exemplary outcome of Christ's transforming love. Paul writes to the Ephesians: '. . . Christ loved the church and gave himself up for her, in order to make her holy by cleansing her with the washing of water by the word, so as to present the Church to himself in splendor . . . So that she may be holy and without blemish' (Eph 5:25–27). In her the Church finds expressed what it is called to be.

The beginning and end of her being in Christ—her Immaculate Conception and her Assumption into glory—crystallise the transforming grace at work in all lives: 'Blessed by the God and Father of our Lord Jesus Christ, who . . . chose us in Christ before the

foundation of the world to be holy and blameless before him in love'
(Eph 1:3–4). The Church, united with the Mother of the Redeemer,
contends with the antagonistic powers of the world to be itself 'a great
portent in the heaven: a woman clothed with the sun, with the moon
under her feet, and on her head a crown of twelve stars. She was
pregnant and crying out in birth-pangs in the agony of giving birth'
(Rev 12:1–2). In her Assumption faith glimpses the 'opened heaven'
of Jesus' promise to the disciples in his conversation with Nathanael:
'Amen, amen, I say to you, you will see heaven opened and the angels
of God ascending and descending on the Son of Man' (Jn 1:51). Her
Son opens the realm of God from above; and Mary, one of us here
below, has gone before into the Father's house (Jn 14:1–3).

Within the jumbled chaos of this community of saints and
sinners, the creed confesses the Church as holy. As always, is a matter
of adoring, in the humility and hope characteristic of Christian
realism, the Holy Spirit working within the Church. For the Church is
fundamentally holy only because God is holy. At the depths of its life,
the Church inhales and breathes forth the Holy Breath of the Father
and the Son. Such holiness does not fail: it is the inexhaustible source
of the Church's grace realised in the Spirited company of Mary and
the 'holy ones', the saints, whose influence precedes and accompanies,
sustains and blesses the often sorry efforts of the Church in any era.

Belief in the one *holy* Church is an especially contentious issue
today. Never before has the vast historical reality of the Christianity
been studied in all the light and darkness of its different periods.
The results tempt many to disillusionment in the face of the human
imperfection that is all too visible. At such times we must ask ourselves
whether we have become all too 'docetic' in our appreciation, not only
of the genuine humanity of Jesus, but also of the historical humanity
of the Church, and even of human reality of ourselves. Still, there is
room for second thoughts. After all, it is only in the Church, through
the sorry reality of very human Christian believers, that we have come
to know Christ, to celebrate his presence, to eat and drink his reality,
to receive his Spirit and hear his word in the inspired scriptures—and
receive his Mary as our Mother in faith. In all that she has received
and now is for us, Mary is the living, acting symbol of another, often
forgotten dimension, the God-given holiness of the Church. Scandal
or impatience can often give rise to the question, 'Are we looking at
the whole reality of the Church?'. It could be that we have become

so censoriously fixated in some distorted fragment of the ecclesiastic reality—as it appears in a particular time or place or person – that the holiness of the Church drops from the frame of reference? Scandal can be a convenient excuse for not being involved in the flesh-and-blood history of faith—with all its demands, risks and ambiguities— by hiding behind our own projections of unliveable excellence. More seriously still, there is the temptation simply to inventing a private sanctity or personal spirituality based on self-justification, set apart from and even against the corporate, pilgrim existence as the Church? A disaffected spirituality comfortably living *off* the Church is eventually faced with the demand to live *for* it. Perhaps Mary's role today is to help us all keep that sense of proportion that is never far from a sense of humour, a forgotten aspect of gift of the joy that no one will take from you (*Cf* Jn 16:22–24). The creed's confession of the 'holy Church' at very least presents the possibility that the grace of God is far more humanly incarnate in our midst than any precious, irritated moralism can perceive. Here, a deeper theology of Mary's place in the communion of saints will help all move closer to the heart of what the Church is and is meant to be. She is not a compensation for our lack of holiness, but an embodiment of the holiness we are being called to receive and communicate: 'Holy Mary, Mother of God, pray for us sinners, now, and at the hour of our death'.

Mary place in the Church of the Third Millennium is illuminated by recalling her relationship to the millennium that preceded her. She stood then at a crucial turning point. The faith of Israel was about to waken to a new universality. As the Gospel of John records, Jesus spoke to the Samaritan woman in order to awaken her to a faith that would not be centred 'neither on this mountain nor in Jerusalem', but in the worship of the Father 'in Spirit and in truth' (Jn 4:21–23). Nonetheless he affirmed, speaking as a son of Israel, 'You worship what you do not know; we worship what we know, for salvation is from the Jews' (Jn 4:22). In the Gospel of Luke, Mary herself proclaims, in her praise of the Lord, that 'He has helped his servant Israel, in remembrance of his mercy, according to the promise he had to our ancestors, to Abraham and his descendants forever (Lk 1:54–55). The ecstatic prayer of the Spirit-endowed Simeon echoes both her assurance of the universality and the historical particularity of the gift she holds in her arms, '. . . My eyes have seen your salvation . . . a light for revelation to the Gentiles and for glory to your people Israel'

(Lk 2:30–32). And it should not be forgotten that while certain of the authorities of his own people brought about the death of Jesus, it was one of his own who was his Mother, and those of his own people who proclaimed his resurrection and preached his Gospel throughout the world. In this light, Mary is for the Church, the New Israel, a precious link with its past, and an inspiration for continuing reconciliation with the Jewish people of today.

Finally, the creed confesses the love of God as leading to 'the life of the world to come': 'God is love' in bringing creation to its fulfilment. The love of God that had time for the emergence of the world and for the whole drama of human freedom will reach the final moment of its communication 'so that God may be all in all' (1 Cor 15:28). God is love, to use a theological term, 'eschatologically'. In this regard, we have already referred to Mary's assumption, the realisation in her in a full-bodied way of eternal life. Here, as in all else, Mary receives from Christ. Ambrose of Milan sums up the cosmic sweep of the mystery of Christ: 'In Christ's resurrection the world arose. In Christ's resurrection, the heavens arose; in Christ's resurrection the earth itself arose'.[8] Related to this universal transformation, the Catholic doctrine of Mary 'assumed body and soul into heaven', has special significance. For the Assumption of Mary is a concrete symbol of the creativity of our God-charged world. Early patristic theology thought of Mary as the New Eve, formed from the New Adam (*Cf* Gen 2:21–13), as the 'mother of all the living'. In such a context, the Assumption is not one more unique Marian privilege. As now assumed into the glory of Christ, she is the anticipation of the heaven of a transfigured creation.[9] She is the paradigm instance of creation open to, collaborating with, the creative mystery of God in Christ. As the Mother of Christ, she symbolises the generativity of creation as it is penetrated by the Spirit: in her, as the Advent antiphon has it, 'the earth has been opened to bud forth the Saviour'. Her Assumption nourishes hope with an assurance that our nature and our history have already, in her, reached their term. She embodies the reality of our world as having received into itself the mystery that is to transform the universe in its entirety. The seer of the Apocalypse invites us to

---

8.   *De excessu fratris sui*, bk 1. *PL* 16, 1354.
9.   See Karl Rahner, 'The Interpretation of the Dogma of the Assumption', in *Theological Investigations I*, translated by C Ernst (London: Darton, Longman and Todd, London, 1961), 215–227.

share his vision of 'the holy city, the new Jerusalem, coming down out of heaven from God, prepared as a bride adorned for her husband' (Rev 21:1–3). With him too we hear the loud voice from the throne saying, 'He will dwell with them as their God, and they shall be his people, and God himself will be with them; he shall wipe away every tear from their eyes. Death will be no more; mourning and crying and pain will be no more, for the first things have passed away' (Rev 21:3-4). In Mary's assumption into glory our world is open to heaven, and the great cosmic marriage begins. In Mary the Spirit has brought forth the particular beauty of creation in the sight of God. In her, our history has come to its maturity, its age of consent, to surrender to the transcendent love for which it was destined. Out of such a union, the whole Christ of a transfigured creation is born. Thus, while the focus of Christian hope is in Christ's death and resurrection, in Mary we have a *reprise* of the paschal mystery in which the gift of transforming grace has already been received and assimilated by the human world.

In reference, then, to seven key Christian terms, *Father, Son Cross, Resurrection, Spirit, Church and eternal life,* we have been sketched the significance of Mary's presence to the Church, and the meaning of doctrines about her and of symbols expressive of her within the matrix of the most fundamental of all Christian affirmations: 'God is Love'. She gives because she has received; and she gives because her giving is an intimate dimension of the tender, human economy of 'the Gift of God' (Jn 4:10). Situated in such a matrix, and never outside it, all she is confessed to be derives from and throws light on the 'Love-Life' that God is and wills us to share in. In communion with her, believers are more sensitised to the immensity of the mystery of mercy into which we have been drawn:

> Therefore lift up your drooping hands and strengthen your weak knees and make straight paths for your feet, so that what is lame may not be put out of joint, but rather be healed. Pursue peace with everyone, and the holiness without which no one will see the Lord . . . You have not come to something that can be touched, a blazing fire, and a darkness, and gloom, and a tempest and a sound of a trumpet, and a voice that made the hearers beg that not another word be spoken to them . . . But you have come to Mount Zion and the City of the Living God, to the heavenly Jerusalem, and to innumerable angels in festal gathering, and to the assembly of the first-born who

are enrolled in heaven, and to God the judge of all, and to the spirits of the righteous made perfect, and to Jesus, the mediator of a new covenant, and to the sprinkled blood that speaks a better word than the blood of Abel (Hebrews 12:12–14; 18–24).

In short, Mary, the *Theotokos*, the God-bearer, makes us more at home in the Father's house (John 14:2).

Mary and A Poet—Gerard Manley Hopkins

A contemporary world-view and sensibility are opposed to the language of the *Magnificat*: 'My soul glorifies the Lord, my spirit rejoices in God my saviour; he looks on his servant in her lowliness; henceforth all generations will call me blessed.' Miriam, a young Jewish woman twenty centuries ago was the antithesis of everything the idols stood for. Her God 'puts forth his arm in strength, and scatters the proud hearted. He casts the mighty from their thrones and raises the lowly'. The void in the lives of the 'proud-hearted' and 'mighty' ones would unleash ever more demonic efforts to fill the emptiness with victims? Would the faith of Israel end in the gas-chamber and ovens of Auschwitz, or does this Miriam, this daughter of Israel, speak more truly: 'He protects Israel his servant, remembering his mercy, the mercy promised to our fathers, to Abraham and his seed forever'. History continues to vacillate at the point of crisis. On the one side, there are the idols of race, greed and power driven by the demons of the seven deadly sins, with an imagination fixed on self-promotion, revenge, and haunted with the dread of death. On the other side, there is another realm of life, and another language spoken by this woman: Praise and humility, a joyful confidence in the God of marvellous impossibilities, a universal hope for divine mercy, the role of the God's servant in the world.

So much of culture is imitation; and so much of that imitation consists in wanting what others want. The envious desire to be like others coveting their power, their fame, their possessions, their security, their beauty, their independence. By being drawn into such patterns of cultural imitation—and modern advertising knows a lot about this—we make the idols that have demanded so much human sacrifice throughout history. The influence of Mary in the

life of faith works chiefly to inspire us to enter this other world of
desire. All the references to her scattered through the Gospels tell
something of her desire. Listen to her *Fiat* at the Annunciation, to
the Magnificat. Consider how she pondered the mystery in her heart;
and her unquestioning faith at Cana when her final words recorded
in the Gospel of the Word are 'Do whatever he tells you' (Jhn 2:5)—
with the result that the water is changed into wine, a sign of a world
transformed by his coming. Look at her at the foot of the cross and
waiting with the disciples at the first Pentecost. All these references
form a certain *Gestalt*. She is, in body and heart, given over to that
transforming grace which is at once a judgment on the world and
the advent of its salvation. Her own grace within this universal grace
is articulated in the solemn Marian doctrines of the Church: her
Immaculate Conception, Divine Maternity, and Assumption into
heaven; and, less formally, expressed in that procession of feasts that
bring into Christian consciousness her exemplary role in and for the
Church as the words of her Son continue to resonate in Christian
lives from generation to generation: 'Woman, behold, your son!';
'Behold, your Mother!'. If Jesus is the desire and imagination of God
incarnate among us, Mary embodies, in her womb and in her heart,
a desire conformed to his desire; and an imagination living from her
Son's way of imagining his Father and the coming Kingdom. The
desire of the world has been confronted by Jesus' example and new
commandment: 'For I have set you an example, that you should do as
I have done to you' (Jn 13:15).

What then does Mary mediate in her role in the economy of grace
and in the imagination of that grace in community of faith? Granting
the emphasis of Vatican II, one can hardly deny that Mary incarnates
the holiness and creativity of the Church itself. Within the Church,
she is a symbol *for* the Church, the presence of what the Church is
destined to be. But there is a deeper level. As *Theotokos*, as the God-
bearer, as the Mother of God, Mary is a unique mediator of the
meaning of the trinitarian love of God. As we relate to Mary given to
us as our mother by the crucified Jesus, we come to a deeper sense our
ultimate identity as God's children.

This is exactly what the Jesuit poet Gerard Manley Hopkins was
getting at in his great Marian poem, '*The Blessed Virgin compared to
the Air we Breathe*'. On that May Day holiday at the Jesuit school at
Stonyhurst in 1883, Hopkins put up his poem on the notice board,

among what he describes as other 'polyglot poems in honour of the BVM'. No doubt this poem, rated by one eminent authority as 'the most penetrating and beautiful Marian poem in our language', was lucky to survive when the notices were taken down . . .

As the title of the poem expresses it, Mary is compared to the air we breathe, 'wild air, world-mothering air,/ Nestling me everywhere/ . . . This needful, ever spent/ and nursing element;/ My more than meat and drink/ my meal at every wink.'

Influenced by the Saints Bernard and Louis Grignon de Montfort, Hopkins finds in the life-giving atmosphere of this planet an analogy of Mary's gracious presence: 'Now but to breathe its praise/ Minds me in many ways/ of her who not only God's infinity/ dwindled to infancy/ Welcome in womb and breast/ Birth, milk and all the rest/ But mothers each new grace/ That does now reach our race–.'

Reflecting on her presence, he writes, 'I say that we are wound/ With mercy round and round/ As if with air: the same/ Is Mary, more by name./ She, wild web, wondrous robe/ Mantles the guilty globe.'

In all this she serves the mystery of Christ rescuing humanity rom the violence of our history, to continue in us his incarnation: 'And plays in grace her part/ About man's beating heart,/ Laying, like air's fine flood,/ The death-dance in his blood;/ Yet no part but will/ Be Christ our Saviour still./ Of her he took flesh:/ He does take fresh and fresh,/ Though much the mystery how/ Not flesh but spirit now/ And makes, O marvellous/ New Nazareths in us.'

By breathing this Marian atmosphere, in which the mystery of the incarnation is continued, a new human identity is formed as, 'Men may draw like breath/ More Christ and baffle death;/ Who born so, comes to be/ New self and nobler me/ in each one and each one/ More makes, when all is done/ Both God's and Mary's Son.' In that cosmic, womb-like air, the whole Christ is brought to birth. The englobing presence of Mary is the matrix in which the meaning of our faith is realised.

In the second section of the poem, Mary figures in Hopkin's poem as an aspect of God's tender incarnation among us. For the poet, when the sky is most blue, the world is most full of light 'When every colour glows/ Each shape and shadow shows.' Her role is make the divine 'Much dearer to mankind;/ Whose glory bare would blind/ Or less would win man's mind./ Through her we may see him/ Made sweeter, not made dim,/ And her hand leaves his light/ Sifted to suit our sight.'

The poem concludes in a more directly prayerful mode: 'Be thou then, O thou dear/ Mother, my atmosphere/ . . . Stir in my ears and speak there/ Of God's love, O live air/ Of patience, penance prayer/ World-mothering air, air wild/ Wound with thee, in thee isled/ Fold him, fold fast thy child.'

Mary is best known in the poetry and feeling of faith. She is at once a pervasive presence and a many-sided symbol. We appreciate this point only by f we set our feeling for Mary as the icon of trinitarian love in contrast with a world of other feelings and other images: soured, bitter, violent, vindictive feelings; and images of a world nourishing itself on its own illusions, serving its own idolatrous projections, exhausted in its own fragile self-glorification.

But Mary breathes a purer air and lives in another atmosphere. To express such an awareness, 'devotion' is now too weak a word—as though it were suggesting something peripheral to the Church's life; a mere consolation for the non-intellectual, something vulgar and deviant. But 'the heart has its reasons . . .' In the feeling of faith, and in its poetry, I think we will find her; more to the point, will find her with those who most suffer and feel overwhelmed by life and even religion itself. Theologians might defer to the poets, and to the simple faithful who have not learned how to doubt, to those whose hopes stretch beyond words, to the peacemakers and the bringers of mercy, to those who love outstrips all ideologies ; and to this woman who stands with us, and directs our gaze into that realm where 'the fire and the rose are one'—to 'the love that moves the sun and the other stars' (Dante).

The *Salve Regina* ends with three untranslatable words: *O clemens, O pia, O dulcis Virgo Maria*—showing our need for poets!

CPSIA information can be obtained
at www.ICGtesting.com
Printed in the USA
JSHW021517150723
44805JS00002B/132